Information Communication

Synthesis Lectures on Information Concepts, Retrieval, and Services

Editor

Gary Marchionini, *University of North Carolina, Chapel Hill*

Synthesis Lectures on Information Concepts, Retrieval, and Services publishes short books on topics pertaining to information science and applications of technology to information discovery, production, distribution, and management. Potential topics include: data models, indexing theory and algorithms, classification, information architecture, information economics, privacy and identity, scholarly communication, bibliometrics and webometrics, personal information management, human information behavior, digital libraries, archives and preservation, cultural informatics, information retrieval evaluation, data fusion, relevance feedback, recommendation systems, question answering, natural language processing for retrieval, text summarization, multimedia retrieval, multilingual retrieval, and exploratory search.

Information Communication
Feicheng Ma

Social Media and Library Services
Lorri Mon

Analysis and Visualization of Citation Networks
Dangzhi Zhao and Andreas Strotmann

The Taxobook: Applications, Implementation, and Integration in Search: Part 3
Marjorie M.K. Hlava

The Taxobook: Principles and Practices of Building Taxonomies: Part 2
Marjorie M.K. Hlava

Measuring User Engagement
Mounia Lalmas, Heather O'Brien, and Elad Yom-Tov

The Taxobook: History, Theories, and Concepts of Knowledge Organization: Part 1
Marjorie M.K. Hlava

Information Communication
Feicheng Ma

ISBN: 978-3-031-01165-8   print
ISBN:978-3-031-02293-7   ebook
ISBN: 978-3-031-03421-3   epub

DOI 10.1007/978-3-031-02293-7

A Publication in the Springer series
SYNTHESIS LECTURES ON INFORMATION CONCEPTS, RETRIEVAL, AND SERVICES #41
Series Editor: Gary Marchionini, University of North Carolina, Chapel Hill

Series ISSN 1947-945X Print 1947-9468 Electronic

Information Communication

Feicheng Ma

Centre for Studies of Information Resources, Wuhan University, China

SYNTHESIS LECTURES ON INFORMATION CONCEPTS, RETRIEVAL, AND SERVICES #41

ABSTRACT

This book introduces fundamentals of information communication. At first, concepts and characteristics of information and information communication are summarized. And then five classic models of information communication are introduced. The mechanisms and fundamental laws of the information transmission process are also discussed. In order to realize information communication, impediments in information communication process are identified and analyzed. For the purpose of investigating implications of Internet information communication, patterns and characteristics of information communication in the Internet and Web 2.0 environment are also analyzed. In the end, case studies are provided for readers to understand the theory.

KEYWORDS

information communication, information communication model, information communication mechanism, law of information transmission, information communication impediments, information communication practice

Contents

Preface

In October 2014, Professor Gary Marchionini and I were invited to participate in the Information Acquisition and Knowledge Service Conference hosted by Nanjing University of Science and Technology. We had met twice before but the tight schedule made it impossible for close contact or talk. This time we had more chance to communicate. Professor Marchionini told me that he was editing a book series for library and information science and teaching of related majors. He invited me to write one of the series, telling me that I can choose the topic by myself. Professor Marchionini is a world-renowned scholar in the field of library and information science, mainly devoted to the teaching and research of information retrieval, information behavior and information services, and he is highly influential in the international circle of library and information science. I accepted his offer delightedly.

The books of the series are not very voluminous, each containing about 70 pages in English, while the content is highly concentrated and dedicated to a specified topic. After thinking it over, I decided to choose "information communication" as the topic of my book. On one hand, it is less likely this topic will be covered by others; on the other hand, this part has been covered in our school's course of "Fundamentals of Information Management," and I have done much research and gained a lot of teaching experiences in this area. Moreover, it is a very unique topic in the context of the Internet. Professor Marchionini also thought highly of this idea after receiving my table of contents. After three months of effort, I completed the book and sent it to Professor Marchionini. He responded promptly and positively, and provided many valuable suggestions. Based on these suggestions, I further perfected my book, and gave explanations where I did not change it accordingly.

Information communication is a fundamental phenomenon in human society, as well as one of the ways in which interactions and connections between humans are realized. It is an important subject in the field of Library and Information Science. This book can serve as a textbook of Library and Information Science for researchers and senior students.

This book covers topics on concepts, models, mechanisms, realization and barriers, and application of information communication as well as basic laws of information transmission.

Chapter 1 elaborates on the concept, characteristics and classification of information. It also emphasizes the relationships among data, information and knowledge in an information chain. Chapter 2 focuses on the basic concepts of information communication, including its classification, implications, user's information behaviors and components of information communication. Chapter 3 reviews five models of information communication: the Shannon-Weaver model of communication, Harold D. Lasswell's 5W formula, Wilbur Schramm's model, Vickery's S-C-R model and Mikhailov's model of scientific information exchange. Chapter 4 discusses the mechanisms of information communication. Information communication can be classified into two types: direct information communication and indirect information communication. For both types, information is typically transmitted in four modes: multi-directional proactive mode, unidirectional proactive mode, multi-directional passive mode and unidirectional passive mode. Chapter 5 introduces two fundamental laws of the information transmission process: the conservation of information and the diffusion of information. The former describes the conservation of information volume, while the latter describes the diffusion of information content in the process of transmission. Chapter 6 demonstrates the process of realizing information communication. The barriers are information variance, information disorder and fidelity and redundancy of transmission, which have varying effects on the realization of information communication. Last but not least, Chapter 7 analyzes the patterns and characteristics of information communication in the Internet context. The activities, tools and applications of information communication, especially the two contexts of Web 2.0 and the mobile Internet are discussed.

There are four case studies at the end that will help illustrate the theoretical models. After illustrating theories and implications of Six Degrees of Separation and Small World in Case 1, a number of typical social network sites, such as Facebook, Foursquare, Mydeveloperworks, Barcode Hero and some China-based websites like WeChat, Renren, Kaixin, 19lou, Traveler365, etc., are presented in Case 2. Characteristics and features of Wikipedia are expounded in Case 3 from the view of collaborative information communication. Microblogs including Twitter and a couple of Chinese microblogging platforms are introduced as examples of network communication tools in Case 4. Each case study ends with an "issue and consideration" section to list issues for further study and consideration.

I hope this book will help those who are interested in information communication obtain basic knowledge on this subject.

The author of this book would like to express special thanks to Professor Gary Marchionini, the series editor for his valuable suggestions and contributions. This book would not have been possible without his help. In addition, we would also like to thank Diane D. Cerra from Morgan & Claypool Publishers for her hard work.

Acknowledgments

This book is suported by the Key International Cooperation Program of the National Natural Science Foundation of China (Program No. 71420107026). I'd like to show my thanks to Dr. Feng Chengjun and Dr. Song Enmei for the valuable materials they provided, and I would also like to express my gratitude to my students Zhao Yiming, Chen Ye, Cao Qian and Yuan Yaqian, etc. for editing the draft and proofreading the book.

CHAPTER 1

On Information

1.1 CONCEPT OF INFORMATION

"Information" is one of the most frequently and widely used words in modern society. It is not only widely adopted by the various aspects and domains of human social life, but also frequently used in the study of natural sciences both biological and non-biological. There is no commonly accepted definition for information; some typical definitions are presented below.

- Information is information. It is neither matter nor energy.

- Information is the difference between things.

- Information is complexity of the system.

- Information is a representation of interactions between things.

- Information is a universal property of matter, and a universal form of connections between things.

- Information is nonuniformity of the temporal and spatial distribution of matter and energy.

- Information is news not known by the receiver beforehand.

- Information is that which eliminates uncertainties.

- Information is that which causes probabilistic distributions to change.

- Information is negentropy.

- Information is a measure of orderliness.

- Information is reflected difference.

- Information is a name for what is exchanged during interactions between humans and their environment.

- Information is that which has an effect on human sense organs.

- Information is the methods and degrees of freedom of choice.

- Information is the content of communication.

- Information is the raw material that is processed into knowledge.

- Information is control instructions.

- Information is intelligence required by decision-making.

- Information is messages.

- Information is signals.

- Information is data.

- Information is experience.

- Information is documentation.

- Information is knowledge.

Some of these definitions are philosophers' attempts to describe information's fundamental properties; some focus on the forms information assumes during its transmission, and some describe its effects on the receiver. While a broader definition for information may encompass all information that is created, transmitted and utilized in both the natural world and human society, our study is mostly concerned with information in human society. In pre-modern days, human understanding of information was limited to the utilization of messages. With the development of human society and sciences, different understandings of information began to be developed in different disciplines.

Communication science is the earliest discipline to view information as an object of study. Because communication, by its very nature, is transmission of information, communication scientists need to examine the nature and measurement of information in order to solve the problems they encountered. "Transmission of Information," by Ralph Vinton Lyon Hartley, published in *Bell System Technical Journal* in 1928, became a foundational work (Hartley, 1928). In this paper, Hartley viewed information as choices of symbols used in communication, and used the number of possible choices for a symbol sequence to measure the amount of information. He proposed that the information being sent is the precise configuration of symbols (which the sender has chosen from a list of symbols). Twenty years later in 1948, Claude Elwood Shannon published "A Mathematical Theory of Communication" in *Bell System Technical Journal* (Shannon, 1948). Using probability theory, he examined several basic theoretical problems in communication, proposed the methods and generalized formulas for computing source information volume and information channel capacity, and obtained a set of theorems regarding transmission of information. For the purpose of quantitative measurement of information, Shannon defined information as reduction of scholastic uncertainty, in other words, information is that which can be used to reduce uncertainties. Based on this thinking, Léon Nicolas Brillouin pointed out that information is negative entropy, or negentropy. On the other hand, Norbert Wiener, the founder of cybernetics, viewed information as the content of generalized communication. In *The Human Use of Human Beings: Cybernetics and Society* (1950), he wrote: "information is a name for the content of what is exchanged with the outer world as we adjust to it, and make our adjustment felt upon it. The process of receiving and of using information is the process of our adjusting to the contingencies of the outer environment, and of our living effectively within that environment." Wiener clearly saw the exchange of information between humans and their environment as a generalized form of communication, which encompasses the information transmission and exchange between human and human, machine and machine, machine and natural world, or human and natural world. Wiener also interpreted information as negentropy. He observed, "Just as entropy is a measure of disorganization, the information carried by a set of messages is a measure of organization. In fact, it is possible to interpret the information carried by a message as essentially the negative of its entropy."

The research into information done by communication scientists yielded significant results. Here, information is viewed as a measure of orderliness (or degree of organization) and as negentropy, which can be utilized to reduce uncertainties. This is an understanding shared by Shannon, Wiener and Brillouin (Hartley's definition being only a special case of Shannon's definition). This is a much deeper and richer view than seeing information as merely messages or content of communication.

Life sciences also began to see the signal exchanges present in the kingdoms of animal and plant, or from a cell to another cell within an organism, or from one organism to another organism, as transmissions of information. For example, the passing down of genetic information over generations through self-replication of nucleic acids (DNA and RNA) has been seen as an important form of information transmission. In the late 1980s, the rapid increase of genome sequencing data resulted in the birth of a new interdisciplinary science, bioinformatics, which utilizes information science to examine the storage, transmission and interpretation of information in organisms and biological processes, analyze the biological information found in the physiological, pathological and pharmacological processes of cells, tissues and organs and facilitate the acquisition, processing, storage, retrieval and analysis of data in biological experiments.

After World War II, collection of scientific information has become an important component of science-related lines of work. Information services for science and technology have developed into an important sector in social and economic life. Coming into the 21st century, the leading role of scientific innovation has been firmly established, and scientific information has been viewed as the most basic resources and prerequisites for scientific and technological research and innovations. For science and technology workers, information includes resources such as scientific research, technological innovations, industrial inventions, investigation reports, patents and standards. The scientific information agencies are responsible for providing information retrieval services to the general public, and providing specialized services to researchers, businesses and governments, such as searching for new inventions, evaluation of research projects, propagation of scientific knowledge, formulation of science strategies and consultation for policies.

In the field of economics, people are usually concerned about information on businesses, commodities (prices), customers and markets. The incompleteness and asymmetry of market information lends value to such information, and enables it to exist as a special type of commodity. As observed by the American economist Kenneth Joseph Arrow (1984) in his *The Economics of Information*, "people may expend labor and financial resources to change the uncertainties they face in the economy and other areas of social life. These changes are the acquisition of information. Uncertainties have economic costs, which makes the reduction of uncertainties a type of profit." Information gains market value due to its effect to reduce uncertainties, which lowers economic costs and increases efficiency. Information streams have become even richer in e-commerce, where they include, in addition to information about buyers, sellers and commodities, also the bidding ranks of suppliers of similar products, advertisements, techniques about how to better utilize the e-commerce systems, on-site search engines, transaction volumes, messages exchanged using IM (*instant messaging*) services, credibility of business participants, etc.

The universal presence and applicability of information has also attracted the attention of philosophers. They realized that, since patterns and characteristics can be found in the forms of existence and states of motion of everything from human thinking and society to the natural world, such forms and states can all be expressed as information. Everything has its inner structure and outer connections, the combined influence of which determines its forms and states. Therefore, information can be said to be a universal property of things.

In everyday usage, information is regarded as experience, knowledge and documentation. Typical definitions expressing this view include, "information is knowledge as the object of storage, transmission and transformation," "information is all knowledge communicated between humans as symbol sequences," "information is experience, knowledge and intelligence required by decisions, plans and actions," and "information is organized and transmittable data." The widespread use of the Internet has brought information into every corner of human life, and no one can deny the ubiquity and indispensability of information. Today, people tend to see information as all the data, symbols, signals and documents being transmitted on the Internet, a massive collection that seemingly contains everything.

Given the brief history of definitions above, we can see that the connotations of information are complicated, and attention must be paid to the conditions and scope of our discussion when talking about the definition of information, with different conditions necessitating different definitions. The definitions we have listed are the results of different people trying to define information from different perspectives under different conditions. By recognizing the conditions under which information can be defined, a clearer understanding can be reached.

In the most general and unspecified sense, we may define information as the forms of existence and states of motion of things.

Here "things" refer to all possible objects in human thinking, society and nature. "Forms of existence" refers to the inner structures and outer connections of things. "Motion" refers to changes in all senses, including all mechanical, physical, chemical, biological, psychological and social movements. "States of motion" refers to the characteristics, phases and patterns demonstrated by things in motion through time and space. As all things have its own forms of existence and states of motion, all things are creating information constantly. This provides the broadest and most generalized definition of information, which can be said to be a fundamental aspect of reality, comparable to matter and energy. We call this information the ontological level.

When we consider that the creation, recognition, acquisition and utilization of information cannot be separated from the subject of knowledge—humanity—and information can only be defined from the perspective of the subject, we may move from the ontological level to the epistemological level. On the epistemological level, information can be defined as: the forms of existence and states of motion of things that are sensed or expressed by the subject of knowledge. Here, what the subject senses is the information input from the outer world to the subject, and what the subject expresses is the information output from the subject to the outer world. Obviously, once the condition of subject is introduced, we begin to narrow down the definition of information.

Comparing the two definitions, we can see that on the ontological level, the existence of information does not require the existence of the subject of knowledge. It is possible to say that information in itself has existed prior to the appearance of humanity, when no humans could have existed to sense, express and utilize information. Contrariwise, on the epistemological level, information cannot be recognized as such without the subject. Thus it can be said that no information existed before the appearance of humanity.

It must be pointed out that the epistemological definition of information has richer connotations than the ontological definition. First, humans as subjects possess sensory abilities, enabling them to sense the existence and motion of things; second, humans possess cognitive capabilities, allowing them to understand the specific meanings in the existence and motion of things; third, humans possess intentionality, and are able to discern the utilities in the existence and motion of things with regard to their intentions. Furthermore, the three aspects are dependent on and inseparable from each other. As a matter of fact, humans must first sense the forms of existence and states of motion of a thing, understand its meanings, and recognize its utilities, and then can they be said to have obtained its information, becoming capable of making correct decisions. We refer to epistemological information that accounts for the external forms, internal meanings and utilities of a thing's forms of existence and states of motion as "comprehensive information," information that only addresses its forms as "grammatical information," information that only addresses its meanings (or content) as "semantic information," and information that only addresses its utilities as "pragmatic information." Epistemological information is comprehensive information, simultaneously concerned with grammatical, semantic and pragmatic information. Information as studied by information theory scholars such as Shannon is pure grammatical information, unconcerned with the meanings and utilities of information.

The ontological and epistemological definitions of information comprise the most basic definitions of information. When we introduce some further conditions upon the epistemological definition, we may obtain more definitions at lower levels of abstraction. The many varied definitions of information listed at the beginning are essentially the results of different conditions introduced when people attempt to understand information from different perspectives.

In this book, we are primarily concerned with the study of social information, which is created, transmitted, exchanged and utilized by humanity's social activities for specific purposes, and includes all languages, symbols, data, messages, experience and knowledge created by humanity and expressed and recorded by other material media. Obviously, everything in this massive system is epistemological information. Information contained within the natural world, organisms and mechanical systems, as long as it concerns human subjects, and is put into service for specific purposes of human society, all falls under our definition of social information. The purpose of this book is to study and solve the problems in the management, exploitation and utilization of this type of information.

1.2   CHARACTERISTICS OF INFORMATION

Having examined the concept of information, we may now further explore the characteristics of information. Conversely, knowing these characteristics may also help us better understand the core concept of information.

1. **The existence of information is universal and objective.** Information represents the forms of existence and states of motion of things. Everything has its own forms of existence and states of motion, which necessitates the information that represents them. The existence and motion of things are universal, thus the corresponding information is also universal. The universal information is absolute and objective. It is absolute, because the physical world has existed prior to the human subject, and the existence of information is independent from the subject. It is objective, because information is not an illusion, but rather can be sensed, acquired, stored, processed, transmitted and utilized by humanity.

2. **The creation of information is ever expanding and infinite.** Everything in the universe has its own forms of existence and states of motion, which create information endlessly. The things that are in the universe are infinitely diverse, endlessly expanding

over space, and changing indefinitely over time. Hence the creation and distribution of information are both infinite. Even within a limited space and time, the things that exist are still infinitely diverse, creating an infinite amount of information.

3. **Information is transmittable over time and space.** While information is created by the existence and motion of things, it can also be separated from its source, and transmitted over time and space. To transmit information over time is to store it, and to transmit it over space is communication—storage being another form of communication, only one that is sent toward the future. Obviously, transmitting information over space also requires time, with the speed of transmission being a limited value; using modern communication technologies, the time required by transmission over space has become shorter and shorter, and can often be omitted. It is vitally important that information can be transmitted over time and space. In human society, it enables not only communications, but also the accumulation and spread of knowledge. As Wiener said, information is the glue that holds human society together. It is impossible to imagine what human society can be without the transmittability of information.

4. **Information is independent from physical media.** Information is a representation of the existence and motion of things, not the things themselves. Such "representations" can be represented using all kinds of symbols, codes and languages invented by humanity, stored using materials from stone and paper to CD-ROM, transmitted using optical, aural and electrical energies. Information cannot exist without such physical media, which indicates a reliance on physical media. However, the nature and meaning of information is the same regardless of the physical media used to represent, record and transmit it, which indicates an independence from physical media. For example, we have a piece of meteorological information about whether it will rain tomorrow. It can be represented using the numbers 0 and 1, or negative and positive electric currents, or even the two sides of a coin; it can be recorded on a piece of paper, a disc or a blackboard; it can be transmitted using light, sound or electromagnetic wave. The choice of these media has no effect on its nature and meaning. That is to say, changing the physical media that carry the information has no effect on this particular representation of an object's forms of existence and states of motion. Due to this property, information can be processed and converted into different forms.

5. **Information is relative to the subject of knowledge.** Since different people have different capabilities for observation, interpretation and understanding, as well as different intentions, the amounts of information they can obtain from the same object are necessarily different. Even supposing their abilities and intentions are entirely the

same, if they observe the same object from different perspectives, the information they obtain will still differ. Based on the objectivity and absoluteness of information, we may suppose the existence information volume in an object X to be a constant I(X). Therefore, the obtained information volume of the ith observer R_i, $I(X, R_i)$ can be expressed as:

$$I(X, R_i) = I(X) - I_0(X, R_i)$$

Since each observer comes with a different volume of prior information $I_0(X, Ri)$, the actual volume of information they can obtain from the object will also be different. This pseudo equation indicates that the obtained information volume depends on the individual observer since observers' prior information may affect information they obtain. This property can be seen everywhere in daily life. To use the equation $E=mc^2$ as an example, physicists are able to see it as a representation of the conversion between matter and energy, while nonprofessionals may only see it as an ordinary equation, or a meaningless combination of numbers and letters.

6. **Information is shareable for its utilizers.** Since information can be separated from its source and its physical media, and is not consumed during its utilization, it is possible for information to be utilized at the same time or at different times by multiple users. The shareability of information is an important characteristic that differentiates it from matter and energy. The utilization of matter and energy takes the form of possession and consumption. If the volume of matter or energy is constant, an overt zero-sum competition will exist between its utilizers. In other words, when utilizing a certain amount of matter or energy, if some people have consumed more of it, the other people would have to consume less or even none of it. This competition is not present in the utilization of information. When someone reads a book, the knowledge content (or *information volume*) she gains from the book would not be affected by the fact that other people had read this book before, nor would it affect other people who will read the book later. In another example, having developed a computer software, the developer may transmit its copies to other users, without losing the information of the software. The utilization of the software by one user does not preclude its utilization by others. The information is shared by the users simultaneously, without any competition.

The shareability of information is one of its fundamental characteristics, with both benefits and disadvantages. On one hand, it means information can be shared as much as possible over both space and time, which can be effective and economic. On the other hand, the simplicity of information sharing also makes the organization and control of intellectual properties in modern information management extremely difficult. This will be discussed in later chapters.

7. **Information is immutable and non-combinable.** Once created, information begins to represent a specific meaning, which is not a simple arithmetic sum of its elements (e.g., symbols, numbers and words). Hence it is impossible to rearrange and recombine these elements arbitrarily without damaging the meaning. Using the expression "the next summer will be hotter than this one" as an example, if the two elements "the next" and "this" switch places, we will get "this summer will be hotter than the next one," which has the opposite meaning of the original information. Only in rare cases can the elements in a piece of information be arbitrarily rearranged and recombined while retaining its meaning. For the same reason, the elements that make up information cannot be arbitrarily removed and separated.

8. **The creation and utilization of information is time-sensitive.** From the perspective of information creation, what information represents are a thing's forms of existence and states of motion in a specific moment. As all things are constantly changing, the object's forms of existence and states of motion will invariably change after the passing of this moment, and the corresponding information will also be different. From the perspective of information utilization, information only has utility at specific moments. On the market, a timely piece of information can be invaluable, enough to revive a dying company; obsolete information is worthless, or may even cause the downfall of a company.

   The time-sensitivity of information does not mean it is better to utilize information as soon as it is produced. While early utilization may help realize the potential of the information, the reverse case is just as common, and some information will increase in value over time like fine wine. The important factor here is "specific moments," as the maximum utility of information can only be realized at the correct times.

The properties discussed above are the basic characteristics shared by all information. In practice, different types of information have their own characteristics. We will leave these for the readers' own analysis.

1.3   CLASSIFICATION OF INFORMATION

Some sort of classification is needed in order to better understand and describe information. Like all things, many different criteria and methods can be used. Commonly, information can be classified:

• by object: natural, biological, mechanical, and social information;

- by nature: grammatical, semantic, and pragmatic information;

- by perspective and process of observation: existence, prior, and obtained information;

- by direction of transmission: vertical, horizontal, and reticulate information;

- by content: economic, scientific, political, cultural, legislative, and entertainment information, etc.;

- by utility: useful, useless, and interference information;

- by operational status: continuous vs. discontinuous information, routine vs. abrupt information, etc.;

- by communication channel: formal vs. informal information;

- by recording method: audio, visual, text, numeral, and algorithm information, etc.; and

- by source: internal vs. external information (e.g., information from within or without the organization), etc.

Obviously, many other criteria can still be used. The purpose of classification is to understand the nature and characteristics of information, in service of its description and utilization; there are no definitive borders between the different categories, and some overlapping will always happen, regardless of our criteria. This is particularly notable when we try to classify information based on its content. For example, if a piece of political or scientific information has a decisive effect on a country or a company's decision to expand into a foreign market, it is at the same time a valuable piece of economic information.

Not all classifications of information are practical, and only a few are of fundamental significance. Classifying information by its nature (grammatical, semantic and pragmatic) is essential to its description, measurement and study in the information sciences, and classifying information, and classifying information by its content, channel and methods of recording is central to the development of information management, services and utilization.

1.4   DATA, INFORMATION AND KNOWLEDGE IN INFORMATION CHAINS

Information can be said to be part of a larger continuum. The information chain is comprised of five elements, fact, data, information, knowledge and intelligence. In simple terms, "facts" are objective reflections of human thought and social activities; "data" are facts that have been digitized, encoded, sequenced and organized into structures; "information" is data that have been represented in media; "knowledge" is information that has been processed, digested, extracted and evaluated; "intelligence" is the capability to utilize knowledge. The upstream of the chain is connected to the physical world, and the downstream is connected to human cognition (Liang, 2003).

In the information chain, information is neighbored by data and knowledge. Through a comparison of the three elements, we can better understand the significance of information.

Data are physical symbols arranged according to certain rules that carry or record information. It can take the form of numbers, text, images, sounds, program code, etc. Our reception of information begins with receiving data; our actual acquisition of information afterward relies on our understanding of the data's context and implicit rules. The context is the information the receiver needs for receiving certain data; when the receiver understands the rules governing the sequences of physical symbols, as well as the commonly accepted object or meaning behind each symbol or symbol combination, the receiver will be capable of obtaining the information carried by a data set, i.e., converting the data into information. This can be represented by the following formula:

Data + Context = Information

Information is the content carried by data. The same information can be represented using different forms of data. For example, you may inform another person of something by telephone call (aural symbols), by letter (text symbols) or by drawing a picture (image symbols). Information tells us "what is conveyed by these symbols." Knowledge is the proper conclusion the receiver obtained from information through processing and deduction. It is humanity's understanding and mastery over the forms and states of human thought, society and nature, acquired through information. It is a systematic collection of information, given a new structure by the human brain through cognitive activities. Knowledge tells us what makes these data meaningful.

The propagation of knowledge generally follows this model:

Knowledge of the Sender → Data → Information → Knowledge of the Receiver

This model shows that in order for knowledge to spread, the sender must first convert her knowledge into data, i.e., physical symbols arranged according to certain rules, which are then transmitted to the receiver via certain channels. If the receiver is capable of understanding the context and rules behind the data, she will be able to receive the information. However, whether the receiver can obtain the knowledge conveyed by the sender depends on the receiver's own information processing and deduction. It is only when the receiver is capable of obtaining proper understandings about objects and the real world that the information has been converted into knowledge. Therefore, the receiver's capability for understanding is crucial in the transformation from information to knowledge.

The capability for understanding is based on the receiver's existing knowledge (e.g., to non-medical personnel, a patient's medical history is only data or information, but to doctors, it contains valuable knowledge). The mechanism through which information is transformed into knowledge can be complicated, but as a general principle, information can only become knowledge when combined with the experience, information and knowledge possessed by the receiver, i.e., the receiver's own context. The formula is:

Information + Experience = Knowledge

For this reason, the acquisition of knowledge is only possible through learning and experiencing (practicing), where our capacity for interpretation and understanding is put to use, so that data can be transformed into information, information into knowledge, old knowledge can be assimilated, and new knowledge can be created.

In the information chain, intelligence is the abilities and strategies for problem solving. It is the ability to work under certain circumstances regarding certain problems and goals, and to achieve the goals by effectively acquiring information, processing information in order to formulate knowledge and strategies and solving problems using the strategies (Zhong, 2002). Intelligence is knowledge animated into action toward certain goals. It is a movement of knowledge under specific conditions.

Based on the information chain schema, we can say that data are the raw materials of information, while information is the raw materials of knowledge; knowledge tends toward becoming the intelligent methods utilized in decision making (Zhang, 2005). The concept of data covers the widest scope, followed by information, then by knowledge. The relationships of inclusion and transformation between the three concepts are shown in Figure 1.1 and 1.2.

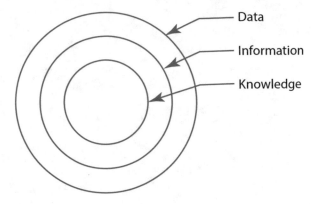

Figure 1.1: Scope of data, information and knowledge.

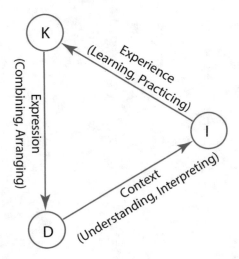

Figure 1.2: Transformation between data, information and knowledge.

Other concepts, such as signals, messages and documentation are only specific units and forms of data, i.e., physical symbols and shells that carry information.

CHAPTER 2

Basic Concepts of Information Communication

2.1 CLASSIFICATION OF INFORMATION COMMUNICATION

Once created, information will be communicated and propagated indefinitely over space and time. The exchange and communication of information can be regarded as one of the most common phenomena in human society and the natural world; as long as something exists and moves, information will be created, communicated and propagated. The communication of information can be categorized as Figure 2.1:

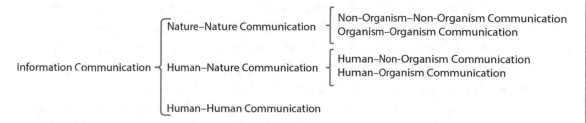

Figure 2.1: Classification of information communication.

Nature-nature information communications are information exchanges and interactions that occur among natural objects, including organism and non-organism, as well as the effects of organism and non-organism on humans. Such interactions follow laws of nature exclusively, with no involvement of human consciousness. The effects of rain, wind and lightning on soil, the communication between birds, the information exchange between animals and minerals and the infection of a virus in a human body all follow laws of nature exclusively. These are pure nature-nature communications, or ontological information communications. In human-nature information communications, only one half of the interaction possesses self-awareness. Spanning across the natural and social worlds, these communications are shaped by the human mind in addition to following laws of nature. For example, scientific research is a form of communication focused around laws of nature, where the information of the natural world is summarized and represented through human understanding, while human labor is a process where information is inputted and imprinted on natural objects under the guidance of the human mind. We may say that scientific research is a process of understanding, where information flows from natural objects toward the human mind, and human labor is a process of shaping the world, where information flows from the human mind toward nature. Human-human information communications, or social communications (which may occur between individuals, organizations or even nations) are interactions between human minds. These are the most complex forms of communication. They depend on the minds and actions of both parties, which are under the influence of certain psychological factors and social rules, as well as connected to other facets of the greater social context. The very system of human society is formed out of these interactions.

2.2   IMPLICATIONS OF INFORMATION COMMUNICATION

Information communications are a basic phenomenon of human society, and a manifestation of interactions and interconnections among humans. For brevity's sake, we will refer to social information communication, this most sophisticated and complex form of communication, as simply "information communication" or "communication."

Communication as traditionally understood is a type of horizontal communication (or synchronic information communication), that is to say, it takes place over a single period in one location, or between several locations. Examples include library or information agency staff providing information to a reader, mass media communicating information to an audience, direct communications between friends, or information exchanges mediated by telephone, telegram, letters or Internet. We would say that the librarian is communicating with the reader, that the information agent is communicating with the user, or that Roosevelt, Churchill and Stalin communicated with each other, but we would seldom think that communication has taken place between a modern reader and Balzac or Tolstoy, even when she is reading *La Comédie Humaine* or *War and Peace*. Nor would we think the librarian or the information agent is communicating with the author or the information source at the same time when they are servicing their customers.

Based on the characteristics of information we have described, we can see now that it is not enough to understand communication as merely taking place horizontally and simultaneously. For a deeper understanding of information in human society, it is necessary to examine information connections in human society that take place vertically between different periods (or diachronic information communication). Thus we may define information communication as the transmission and exchange of information, including knowledge, messages, data, facts, etc., via corresponding symbol systems, between subjects of knowledge (individuals, or organizations formed by individuals) from different positions in time and/or space.

The main function of synchronic or horizontal communication is to overcome the spatial distance between two subjects and facilitate timely information-sharing. The main function of diachronic or vertical communication is to overcome the temporal distance between two subjects, connecting the past and the present, which enables the inheritance and further development of information.

Table. 2.1 depicts the functions and methods of synchronic vs. diachronic communication.

Table 2.1: Methods and media of information communication		
	Information communication	
	Synchronic Communication (over spatial distance)	Diachronic Communication (over temporal distance)
Methods	Internet, fax, telephone, telegram, radio, television, mails, gestures, flag signals, clocks, drumbeat, lights, beacon fires, oral speech, physical objects, etc.	CD-ROMs, floppy disks, audiotapes, video recordings, photographs, paintings, writings, documents, historical buildings, historical artifacts, oral speech, etc.

Each individual must by necessity participate in both synchronic and diachronic communications, as she must both communicate synchronically with contemporary people to acquire and share recent information, and communicate diachronically with earlier generations in order to inherit the knowledge accumulated by humanity. There is no strict difference between synchronic and diachronic communications on a fundamental level, as all communications take place along the arrows of space and time. Telephone is indeed a notable medium for synchronic communications, while documents, artifacts and archaeological digs are media for diachronic communications, but other cases such as oral speech would not be so simple. A conversation between two individuals may be a synchronic communication, however a legend passed down over generations would be a case of diachronic communication.

Modern information technology has not only succeeded in eliminating the spatial distances in communications, but is also in the process of eliminating their temporal distances, which makes it even more difficult to differentiate between synchronic and diachronic communications. For example, the Internet and telephone has made the spatial distance between people unnoticeable, creating the global village, while virtual reality technologies will eventually achieve face-to-face communications between living and historical people, across the distance of time.

Figure 2.2 is a representation of the temporal-spatial relationship between synchronic and diachronic communications:

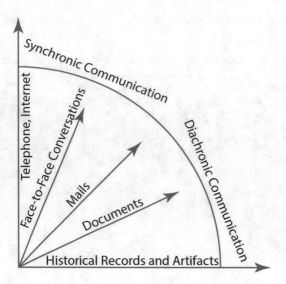

Figure 2.2: Relationship between synchronic and diachronic communications.

No matter which form the communication takes, there must be a sender (S), who is the source and the producer of information, and a receiver (R), who is the final utilizer of information. They can be from different spatial locations in the same period, e.g., in communications among Roosevelt, Churchill and Stalin, or from different spatial locations in different periods, e.g., the thoughts of Balzac and Tolstoy being received by later generations through their writing, or later people learning about Einstein's theory of relativity. In whichever case, the object of communication is the information possessed by the subjects of knowledge.

The process of communication can be direct (e.g., in face-to-face communications) or indirect (e.g., in non-simultaneous or non-face-to-face communications). For indirect communications, some third parties are required to act as intermediaries, creating an information transmission chain. The nodes of the chain can be individuals, publications or other media created and transmitted by individuals, or a mixture of several different media. For example, the theories of Einstein and Newton can be transmitted first through publications (publisher, distributor and library) to scholars, then through the scholars' lectures to a wider audience, thus forming a transmission chain.

Information communication is essentially a unidirectional transmission. A closer look at the process of communication will reveal that the direction of information flow is always from S to R, making it a temporally irreversible process. For example, when the individuals A and B communicate with each other, firstly, A sends information to B, then B sends information to A. These are two information streams in two opposite directions: A→B and B→A.

Since communication requires both parties to be humans with cognitive capabilities, the source of information (from the perspective of R) is necessarily information coming from another person's mind (S), rather than directly coming from observation of nature or society. If we refer to ontological information as objective information, then all information transmitted in communications has been transformed from objective information by the human mind. Such epistemological information is the result of S's cognitive process. We refer to this indirect information as subjective information. Figure 2.3 depicts this process of cognition and information communication.

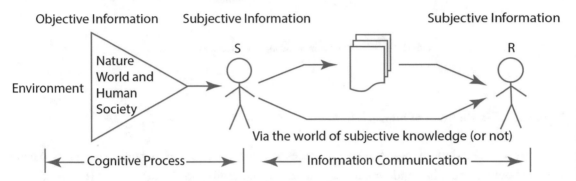

Figure 2.3: Process of cognition and communication.

Information communication also requires intentionality on both sides, i.e., S or R sends or receives the information intentionally. No communication exists when only one party possesses intentionality. That is to say, R must possess the demand for information, and S must possess the intention to provide information.

2.3   INFORMATION COMMUNICATION BEHAVIORS

We can see now that there are two basic concepts in information communication: information and communication. The two concepts are inseparable, as information is that which is communicated, and communication is all about information. Communication is universal in human society, and the behaviors of communications are some of humanity's most basic behaviors.

Since communication involves the subjective information existing in the minds of individuals, the processes of transforming subjective information into objective information and vice versa are required for both the sender S and the receiver R. Using only S's perspective as an example, first one must acquire and generate information through the cognitive process. Like all humanity, one learns about the world through objective information, and one's subjective information is a representation or reflection of some objective information. Afterward, an information output process is required, where information in one's mind is transformed via human behavior into information existing in the external world. Human behaviors may be categorized by their intentionality into intentional and non-intentional behaviors, and intentional behaviors can be further categorized by their relevance to communication into information and non-information behaviors. Information behaviors include speech, writing, gestures, etc., and non-information behaviors include manual labor, operating machinery, etc. (see Figure 2.4).

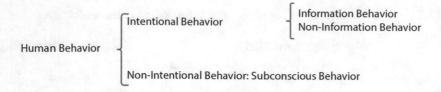

Figure 2.4: Classification of human behavior.

The realization of communication relies on the information behaviors of both parties. We've shown S must be sending out information purposefully; on the other side, R must also act with the purpose of obtaining information. R's behaviors can still be divided into intentional and non-intentional behaviors, and the non-intentional behaviors into information and non-information behaviors. Processes like listening, reading, touching, tasting, smelling, etc., are closely related to reception of information, making them information behaviors; while manual labor, operating machinery, etc., can be related to information, since reception of information is not their intention, they are non-information behaviors.

Combining the communicative behaviors of S and R results in the following categorization (see Figure 2.5):

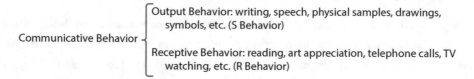

Figure 2.5: Classification of communicative behavior.

2.4   COMPONENTS OF INFORMATION COMMUNICATION

Information communication is a social process, and certain conditions and elements are required for its realization. These conditions and elements can be summarized as:

1. **Sender.** Also called the transmitter or producer of information. It is the initial source of information, as well as the first link on the information transmission chain. It is

generally not used to refer to intermediaries of the transmission process, such as information agencies, libraries, document centers, etc.

2. **Receiver.** Also called the receptor. It is the final receiver or utilizer of information.

3. **Communication channel.** The channels through which information reaches the receiver. No matter the channels, and no matter what sophisticated technologies they have employed, the most basic channels for S and R remain their sense organs: their abilities to see, hear, taste, smell, feel, and other channels or technologies function only as measures to expand, extend or transform these senses.

4. **Symbol system.** It is the carrier of information during communication. It includes speech, writing, gestures, facial expressions, tokens, beacon signals, flag semaphores, computer code, etc. It also encompasses the methods and rules through which the symbol elements in a system are organized and arranged.

5. **Knowledge base.** It encompasses all knowledge and information in the human mind, and is both the ultimate source and destination of communication.

6. **Supporting conditions.** These are conditions that ensure the realization of communication, including: (a) natural conditions, such as the effects of light, sound, electricity and air in transmission of information; (b) technological conditions, including technologies for communication, storage, information processing, etc.; and (c) social conditions, i.e., the social system that enables communication, e.g., legislative, policy and economic conditions, existence of information agencies, etc.

CHAPTER 3

Models of Information Communication

Models or schemas of information communication present us with a simplified textual, graphical or procedural description of the communication process, in order to reveal the nature and patterns of communication. They have played a significant role in realizing the potential of information and improving our communication. In this section, some important models of communication will be introduced.

3.1   SHANNON-WEAVER MODELS OF COMMUNICATION

In 1949, Claude Elwood Shannon, the founder of information theory, proposed the most well-known model of communication in *A Mathematical Theory of Communication* (see Figure 3.1) together with Warren Weaver (Shannon, 1948). Their purpose was to solve the problems encountered in communicating between different machines. This model depicts communication as a unidirectional linear process comprised of five steps. The information source is responsible for sending the information to be transmitted, which is encoded by the encoder into a signal format suitable for the channel to be used, arriving at the decoder. The decoder receives the signal, transforms it back into information and delivers it to the destination, i.e., the information sink. Noise refers to all interferences on the correct transmission of information that are unintended by the parties, which may originate from malfunctions in machinery, or external factors. Noise causes information distortion. How to effectively reduce interferences and control distortion are important issues in communication.

The Shannon-Weaver model was designed for signal transmissions between different machines. As an early representation of information theory, it laid the foundations for other, later models of communication, and guided researchers in their study of communication from a technical perspective. The model still suffers from some limitations. For example, it is mainly concerned with grammatical information, rather than pragmatic and semantic information. It is also a unidirectional linear model with no consideration for feedback. For these reasons, it has limited applications in explaining communicative behaviors and processes in human society.

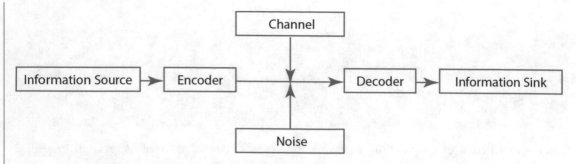

Figure 3.1: The Shannon-Weaver model of communication.

3.2 LASSWELL'S 5W MODEL

In 1948, the American political scientist Harold Dwight Lasswell (1948) published the article "The Structure and Function of Communication in Society," where he formulized the 5W model for analyzing communicative activities in human society (see Figure 3.2), which describes communication using five questions: Who? Says What? In Which Channel? To Whom? With What Effect? The 5W model is a highly influential model that defined the scope for the discipline of communication studies.

In addition to highlighting the sender, the receiver and the channel, this model emphasizes the content of information and the impact of communication, making it effective for analyzing political communications and propaganda. Later in 1958, Richard Braddock expanded the Lasswell model to "7W": Who, Says What, In Which Channel, To Whom, Under What Circumstances, For What Purpose, With What Effect.

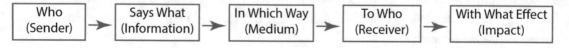

Figure 3.2: The Lasswell's 5W model.

3.3 SCHRAMM'S MODEL

The American scholar of mass communication Wilbur Schramm proposed three models of communication in his 1955 article "How Communication Works" (Schramm, 1955). The first model is similar to the Shannon-Weaver model (see Figure 3.3 (a)). In the second model, Schramm built on the first simple model by pointing out that a shared experience is required for both parties in a communication. In other words, real communication only takes place within the range of the shared experience between the source and the information sink, since all signals that can be understood by both parties must necessarily fall within the range (see Figure 3.3(b)). In the third model, Schramm further highlighted the mutual effects on each other between two individuals in communication. According to Schramm, the two sides in a communication both are required to encode the meanings they want to convey into signals, transmit the signals, decode the signals from the other side,and interpret the decoded information in order to create meanings. Thus exchange of information is formed out of a process of transmission and feedback, and the larger process of communication is a repeated feedback loop. This model is focused on the process rather than effect of communication. It reflects the characteristics of interpersonal communication, particularly face-to-face communication, and is not applicable to mass communication. This model is also called "Schramm's feedback loop" (see Figure 3.3(c)).

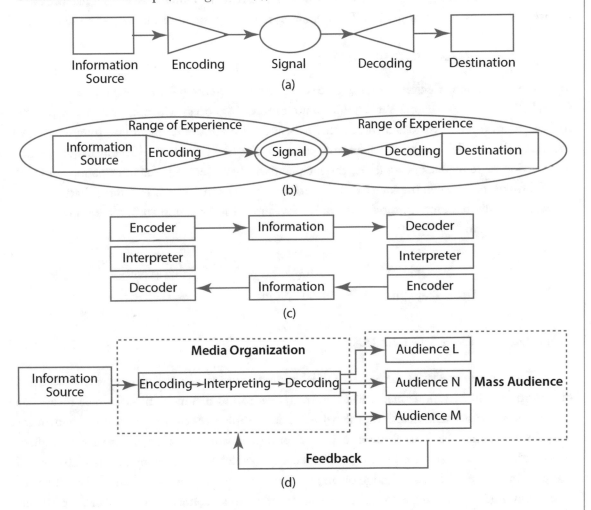

Figure 3.3: Schramm's model.

Schramm also developed a model of mass communication. In this model, the two sides of communication are the mass media and their audience. The mass media functions as an agent of transmission. They receive input from information sources, and then output many mass-produced, identical messages to the audience, which are the targets of communication. The audience is comprised of many individuals, each belonging to one's own social groups, with ongoing communications among individuals, and between individuals and groups. When the audience receives the messages, its members will make decisions based on these messages along with information from other sources, and act upon their decisions, which creates feedback (see Figure 3.3(d)).

The early models of communication are often unidirectional, i.e., a one-way transmission from sender to receiver, while most communications in reality are two-way interactions. The Schramm model introduces the idea of feedback and reframed communication as a feedback loop of interactions between both parties. This is a better representation of real human communications.

3.4   VICKERY'S S-C-R MODEL

The Source-Channel-Recipient model, or S-C-R model of communication, is proposed by Brian Campbell Vickery and Alina Vickery. Communication is a process where information leaves the source, passes through various media or channels, and arrives at the recipient (see Figure 3.4). The source in this model can be individuals or texts. Due to their needs in decision-making, problem-solving or reducing uncertainties, the recipient will have demands for information, and seek out information. Between the source and the recipient, the channel acts as an intermediary. Outside of natural media of communication, the various systems of information are the main instruments of communication.

Figure 3.4: The Vickery S-C-R model.

The three elements of the S-C-R model correspond to the source, channel and destination of information in Shannon's model in form. In comparison to Shannon's model which focuses on communications between machines, the S-C-R model emphasizes communications in human society. In this model, the three elements are all under the influence of society, and its examination of communication must also account for the social context, which includes many factors such as social statuses, and the effects of knowledge on an individual's reception of information. Vickery believed that communication is inherently interactive and mutual, so all connections between the elements of the S-C-R model are two-way movements.

3.5   MIKHAILOV'S MODEL OF SCIENTIFIC EXCHANGE

In the mid-20th century, the American sociologist Herbert Menzel conducted a systematic study on the process of communication from the perspective of information channels, and proposed the model of formal and informal communications. In this model, all social communications can be categorized into formal communication (in legally established organizations, through legally recognized channels, protected by law, required for functioning of social institutions) and informal communication (free and willing information exchanges between members of a society or an informal group). This theory was further developed by the former Soviet information scientist Aleksandr Ivanovich Mikhailov into a generalized model of scientific communication system. Scientific communications are divided into formal and informal communications in the model (see Figure 3.5).

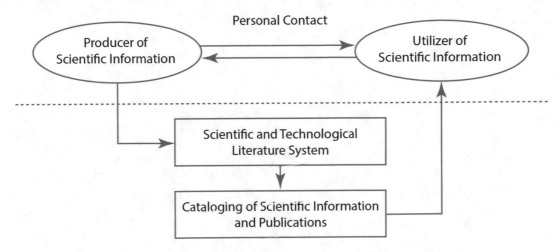

Figure 3.5: Generalized model of scientific communication system.

A formal communication is conducted through a scientific literature system or otherwise under the control of a third party. Its advantages are: the obtained information is highly reliable; detailed and comprehensive information on a topic can be picked up from a massive amount of literature; there is no need to meet the information producer face-to-face. Its disadvantages are: long delays in transmission; and the requirement for skill in searching for information using a literature system. An informal communication is conducted through personal contact between scientists or researchers, such as direct conversations about their works, visiting exhibitions of scientific information, public speeches, exchanging letters, preprints and publications, preparations prior to publishing, etc. Due to a lack of intermediaries, it benefits from: short delays in transmission; acquisition of information can be highly selective and specific; quick feedback; and obtained information can be easily comprehended and properly evaluated. The limitations of informal channels are: difficulty in assessing the reliability and accuracy of information; only a small number of people can participate in direct communications; impossibility to build up an information store for later tasks.

CHAPTER 4

Mechanisms of Information Communication

4.1 FORMATION OF SOCIAL INFORMATION STREAM

Information is one of humanity's basic needs, and humanity will intentionally conduct information communications. Hence once information is produced, it will flow toward certain utilizers or receivers, forming a continuous stream between producers and utilizers of information, i.e., the information stream (see Figure 2.3). Depending on the temporal and spatial locations of S and R, the stream may take different forms, some as brief as a face-to-face conversation, and some over long distances of time or space like a conversation over continents, or a communication from ancient times to the present. Sometimes information flows directly from S to R, sometimes passes through intermediaries like newspapers, broadcast stations, libraries, bookstores, information agencies, etc. (which are information systems in a general sense). However complex the intermediate process is, a thread of information links S to R, which we will refer to as an information transmission chain or a social information stream.

A social information stream, the movement of information from the producer S through (or not) other social nodes to the utilizer R, is a universal phenomenon. The social stream keeps S and R in contact. It can be as simple as a dialog between two individuals, or as complex as the utilization of patented technology, where first the inventor (information producer) must apply for a patent, and the patent document must be printed, distributed to patent centers around the country, and finally delivered to its users. It can be as short as a conversation taking place in a few seconds: "Where are you going?" "To the bookstore." It can also be as long as the millennia-spanning journey of Confucius's philosophy, which was written down by his pupils, made into books, read by scholars, printed into books again, published by a publishing house, distributed by distributors, procured by libraries, borrowed by readers and lectured to students.

Throughout history, social information streams have developed from simplicity to sophistication. Prior to the invention of writing, humanity could only hold conversations within the range of hearing, and the flow of the stream takes place in one short moment. With the appearance of writing and other symbols, the development of information storage and transmission technologies, the constraints of space and time on the spread of information have been gradually lifted. Humanity's need and utilization of information has been becoming more and more social, sophisticated and diverse, and much information would be impossible to transmit from S to R without the processing and transformation of intermediaries. As social information streams grow more sophisticated, greater demands have also been put on the faculties of information control.

4.2   WAREHOUSE OF INFORMATION COMMUNICATION

In addition to S and R, one or more intermediaries are often found in social information streams. They could be editors, publishers, bookstores, libraries, information centers, and TV and radio stations spreading information, or organizations and institutions passing down instructions. These essential intermediaries in communication are the links on the information transmission chain. The stream from an author (S, the information producer) to readers (R, the information utilizer) can be visualized by the following:

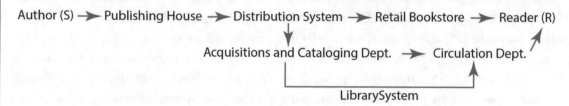

Figure 4.1: Information stream from an author to readers.

By leaving out the names of the nodes, this diagram can be simplified into:

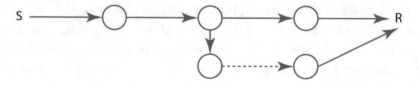

Figure 4.2: Information transmission chain from an author to readers.

In Figure 4.2, the arrows represent information streams, and the circles represent nodes on the information transmission chain. We refer to these nodes as information warehouses. An information warehouse (W) is an intermediary passed by information during its flow from S to R. It must be an individual or a manmade system with the functions of storing, converting, processing and/or transmitting information. Publishing systems, information agencies, broadcast stations and libraries are just a few examples.

We can infer from the definition that except for direct communications between S and R, all communications involve warehouses, which we will refer to as communication without warehouse and communication with warehouse respectively.

Figure 4.3: The warehouse model of information communication.

Because communication is conducted over both time and space, we may also categorize the information warehouses into time and space warehouses. Time warehouses facilitate the transmission of information over time, e.g., archives, museums, libraries, art galleries, information centers, etc. Space warehouses facilitate the transmission of information over space, e.g., newspapers, journals, post system, radio and TV media, computer network, etc. Both have two functions: receiving information from S or the previous warehouse, and processing, converting, storing and/or filtering the information; and sending information to R or the next warehouse.

It should be noted that while R often treats information warehouses as sources of information, warehouses like libraries and information centers are actually intermediate links in communication, and the real, initial sources are the producers S, who are scattered through world history. The purposes of libraries, information centers, data centers, etc., are similar to beacons and relay stations in ancient times in that they are social mechanisms for transmitting information.

Information warehouses are intermediaries of communication, but some warehouses are also utilizers of information. Unlike the post office and the postmen, which have no knowledge about the content of the letter it delivers, they will absorb and make use of the information. For example, an individual A hears that a certain company's stock price will rise. A immediately buys in the stock, and sends this news to a friend B. B does the same, and sends the news to C. Here A and B are both receivers of information and warehouses of communication.

The information warehouse theory reveals the true sources of information as its initial producers, rather than what its utilizers commonly perceive. It also gives us a perspective outside the boundaries of singular disciplines (which have their own perspectives on communication), allowing us to obtain a general understanding of communication's basic mechanism. This theory will serve as the foundation for information management.

4.3   DIRECT COMMUNICATION AND INDIRECT COMMUNICATION

As stated above, based on the presence or not of information warehouses, communications can be categorized into direct communications (without warehouse) or indirect communications (with warehouse). Direct communications are relatively simple processes where the transmission occurs directly between S and R. In indirect communications, due to obstacles between S and R that prevents both parties from direct contact, information warehouses become necessary in the form of social agents.

In communications, social agents (or intermediaries) refer to the phenomenon where either side of a communication (S or R) is unable to directly deliver the information to the other side (R or S), thus the communication is transitioned to an information warehouse in the society, which acts as an agent for S and R to realize the communication. The warehouse is referred to as an agent (A), and a communication with warehouse is also called a communication with social agent. A can be an agent to either S or R. Examples of S's agents include book publishers or technology traders being entrusted by authors or inventors to help them spread their information and facilitate transactions; examples of R's agents include libraries and information agencies being entrusted by users to help retrieve literature or data.

Direct communications and communications with social agents (indirect communications with warehouses) have entirely different characteristics. These differences are:

1. A direct communication takes place directly between S and R. Its medium system is purely natural and objective, with no involvement of social elements, such as direct conversations between S and R, visiting a laboratory, product demonstrations, providing experiment data and report, etc. A communication with social agents requires involvement of social systems like libraries, information centers, etc. Direct communications are vivid and direct, with quick feedback and short delays, which features are absent in communications with social agents.

2. In a direct communication such as a face-to-face talk, the source information (what is provided by S) or demand for information (R's request) are conveyed directly between S and R, without the intervention and control of social systems. In communication with social agents, both the source information and the demand information must pass through A, which often changes the information; e.g., the words used, the mood of the expression and the ideas being emphasized are all affected by A's expression and transformation of information. On the other hand, many dedicated social agent institutions (e.g., publishing houses, news agencies and information systems) serve as supervisors and evaluators of information capable of maintaining standards of quality, while direct communications are more casual and less rigorous.

3. All direct S-R communications are synchronic, while communications with social agents can be both synchronic and diachronic. Diachronic communications can be retrospective or prospective. Indirect communications can transmit information over longer temporal or spatial distances, and can be more efficient through effective matching of S and R.

4. The relationship model is S-R in a direct communication, and S-A-R with a social agent. We can transform an S-A-R relationship into S-R relationships: from R's perspective, A is an agent of S, thus S-A-R = A(S)-R; from S's perspective, A is an agent of R, thus S-A-R = S-A(R). Both the relationships A(S)-R and S-A(R) are direct communications similar to S-R.

5. When multiple agents are involved in a communication, due to their capability for transmission, one can treat an agent node immediately next to any node as representing all the agents that follow it. For example, the information from S is first sent to a publisher, the first agent; the publisher's book is distributed by a distributor, the second agent; the book is circulated by a library, the third agent. From R's perspective, the library can be treated as an agent for the entire social agent system, and the information stream can be viewed as a simple A(S)→R. Similarly, S can also treat the publisher as an agent for the entire communication process, i.e., S→A(R).

4.4   FOUR MODES OF INFORMATION TRANSMISSION

The transmission of information, whether direct (without warehouses) or indirect (with warehouses), generally follow four patterns.

1. **Multi-directional proactive transmission.** In this mode, S or A proactively transmits the information they produced or collected to non-predetermined R, based on the demands of the entire society. Examples include a book distributor sending out catalogs of new books, an information center reporting on secondary documents (or information) selectively and a website choosing information to be pushed to users. Multi-directional proactive transmission is the basic approach in professional information services. Due to the massive volume of primary information, it would be difficult for users (R) to find what they need, and even if they can find it, they would not have the time and energy to read, filter, evaluate and absorb all the information. The professional information services (A) undertake to condense the huge volume of primary information into secondary information for R, thus greatly increasing the efficiency of communication.

In the Internet environment, the number of information resources is growing exponentially and constantly, making fast retrieval of information a difficult task. The catalogs, indices, lists, etc., found on the Internet are examples of multi-directional proactive transmission. While traditional multi-directional transmissions are limited to one agency servicing a geographic region, the Internet has enabled proactive transmissions toward the world, with many additional advantages, including fast speed and short delays, high degree of selectiveness and specialization, quick feedback and vividness of presentation (Zhang, 2002).

2. **Unidirectional proactive transmission.** In this mode, S or A transmits information to a predetermined receiver R, based on their knowledge of user demands. This is the pattern of selective dissemination of information (SDI) services, which delivers timely selected information to users. This pattern often occurs when S or A has long-term close associations with R, and their knowledge of R's demands allow for timely delivery of specialized information.

Unidirectional proactive transmissions are further developed by specialized databases based on user demands in the Internet environment. These databases have aggregated and organized information gathered from wide-ranging sources (including online resources, CD-ROMs, printed documents, etc.), giving users a comprehensive view on the topic. Moreover, their user-tracking feature allows creation of custom user profiles, updated according to user demands. Information that meets each user's search criteria can be periodically aggregated and delivered to their e-mail addresses. These services are more efficient than traditional methods.

3. **Multi-directional passive transmission.** Also called directionless passive transmission. This is another mode without predetermined receivers. It is the pattern of information services open toward a society, such as the services provided by libraries and information centers, and the information websites. While the users who come to libraries, information centers or websites are proactively seeking information, the way these services provide information is passive.

The information services provided by websites involve the website performing selection, evaluation and organization on a large volume of information, and storing the organized information on its pages under certain categories. The library services also require collection, organization and storage of information according to certain sorting criteria for the users' peruse. This is a common pattern of information transmission.

4. **Unidirectional passive transmission.** Also called directed passive transmission, this mode is mainly seen in consultation services provided by S or A. As S or A has no knowledge about who R is and what kind of information they need, they can only provide R with their knowledge, experience and information resources. R may make inquiries about topics such as specific data or facts, and S or A will answer these requests passively, to a specific target R.

A further development of information consultation services is information analysis and prediction. Complex problems such as the general trend of a scientific discipline, or the market share of a product type cannot be answered by a simple lookup. Answering these questions requires detailed research reports containing analysis, comparisons, conclusions and suggestions, made after examining primary and second information, and sometimes conducting local surveys.

In professional information services, the four modes complement each other. Generally, multi-directional transmissions are in service of unidirectional transmissions, providing them with source information, which is delivered by unidirectional transmissions to the final destinations of communication.

Some more comparisons can be made between the modes.

Multi-directional proactive transmission is the most basic and important mode of transmission in professional information services. It forms the core of the workflow in information management and services. Multi-directional proactive transmission necessitates the collection, processing and organization of information, providing a foundation for other types of transmissions. The users' acquisition of information also begins with the information agency's multi-directional proactive transmissions.

Multi-directional transmissions tend to be easier, as unidirectional transmissions are for specific targets, thus requiring A's efforts to understand their specific needs. Proactive transmissions are easier than passive transmission, as there is more time for preparing the information.

Directed transmissions are the ideal of information services, as providing tailored information to specific users maximizes the utility of information. Directed proactive transmission is the most advanced form of information service, as well as the most difficult. By comparison, directed passive transmissions occur more often, and as they are based upon information collected from multi-directional proactive transmissions, it is possible to discover the deficiencies in multi-directional proactive transmissions from them. Improving multi-directional proactive transmissions will benefit all aspects of communication.

In the end, it must be pointed out that each pattern has its purposes in information management and services. Overemphasis on any pattern would upset the balance of the communication system.

CHAPTER 5

The Law of Information Transmission: Conservation and Diffusion

Social information streams are governed by laws that ensure the effective communication of information. The two most basic laws are the conservation and diffusion of information.

5.1 THE CONSERVATION OF INFORMATION

Information conservation describes the maintenance or variation of information during its transmission. For the information producer, every action is accompanied by the creation of new information. Whether the information is recorded, or distorted or attenuated due to external factors, the information itself would never disappear. In other words, once created, information will exist forever, retaining the same volume as the time of its creation. A similar case can be made for the receiver. When information is inputted into our mind, aside from limitations of our sense organs, and other factors that cause us to receive information selectively, our brain has either received the information or not received it. R's information reception is an all-or-nothing process, thus conservation of information also applies to the receiver. For example, when a person has heard about Apollo's moon landing from radio, he has received the information. His memory of it might become fuzzy or forgotten, but we cannot say he has never received the information.

The conservation of information also means that for system A, whose information volume is I_A, the information it possesses will be unchanged after being outputted, i.e., $I_A - I_A = I_A$. For the receiver who has received the information I_A, even if the same I_A is repeatedly transmitted to it, the information it possesses will be constant without increase, i.e., $I_A + I_A = I_A$. This property indicates: information can be shared; when obtaining information, only new information, or the information one does not already possess is needed.

Following the analysis, information conservation can be summarized as: in both production and reception of social information, the existence of information is binary (either 0 or 1); once generated, information can only be concealed, not destroyed; similarly, once received, information can only be forgotten, not become nonexistent.

The conservation of information is a fundamental characteristic of social communication. It is S-information conservation for S, and R-information conservation for R.

For social information streams, S-information conservation means information will exist permanently as soon as it has been outputted from an information producer's mind to the external world. It may be relocated, transformed or concealed, and people may overlook it, or lack the means to receive it, but the information will never be eliminated. This is the reason many historical facts unknown to ancient people can be discovered through modern technology. The law of S-information conservation is the basis for evidence collection in criminal investigations and archaeological research.

R-information conservation describes the binary characteristic of information's reception process, where information is either received or filtered before entering R's mind. In psychological terms, R-information conservation takes place in long-term memories. Any information becomes permanently remembered once it is committed to a person's long-term memory, where it may become commonly used by R, or it may be concealed or forgotten due to lack of use.

Information conservation also encompasses the conservation from input to output, i.e., the conservation of information during a warehouse's transmission. For the information stream $S \rightarrow W_1 \rightarrow W_2 \ldots \rightarrow R$, the output of S is supposed to be the input of R, i.e., conservation in the process transmission, which is the goal social information streams generally strive for. From S's perspective, a message sent out in location a at moment A should not undergo major changes when it reaches location b at moment B. Due to this principle, generally the post office will not open letters, telecom stations will not interfere telephone calls and editors will not alter the intent of an article. Conversely, the message R receives in location b at moment B should also be the same as the one S sent out in location a at moment A. Otherwise, the information streams would distort all information and render social communications meaningless.

As a principle, information warehouses are supposed to ensure the fidelity of information in transmission, and prevent the altering or damage of meaning during its transformation of information. The requirements on information fidelity ensure the conservation of information in transmissions, or T-information conservation.

The laws of S-, R- and T-conservation are general principles of social information streams. In the practice of communications, we may be unable to perceive or realize these principles due to various limitations we work under. This means information conservation is only applicable under limited conditions as a principle.

5.2   THE DIFFUSION OF INFORMATION

The laws of information diffusion, including multi-direction symmetry in information diffusion, and the law of diminishing density in transmission, are rules that govern the information outputted from information source S in social information streams.

5.2.1   MULTI-DIRECTIONAL SYMMETRY IN INFORMATION DIFFUSION

Multi-directional symmetry in information diffusion refers to the property that during the transmission or diffusion of information, if the external medium surrounding source S (including both natural and social media) is homogeneous and uniformly distributed, the diffusion from S will be symmetric on all directions. For example, a bell is rung in a space with air of uniform density. The bell is the information source, and the sound of ringing, as a form of information, is transmitted following the rule of multi-directional symmetry, i.e., the information R will receive is the same on all points with the same distance to S.

Similarly, social information streams also follow the rule of multi-directional symmetry in a homogeneous social medium system. For example, if a lesson is taught by a teacher to students of similar capabilities, and then taught to more students by these students, the spread of the lesson will be similar in all directions. In another example, in a typical governmental system, the structure of institutions and distribution of power are similar between various underlying local governments. Therefore orders from the central government to all county-level local governments will arrive at roughly the same time, carrying the same amount of information.

The multi-directional symmetry of transmission has the following aspects: (a) symmetry of transmission speed; (b) symmetry of content; (c) symmetry of traveled space (or distance); and (d) symmetry of information intensity. For social information streams, symmetry of transmission specd means that information outputted by the source S should have traveled the same distance in any direction after the same amount of time. The "distance" here encompasses not only physical distance, but also social distance. Symmetry of content means that as long as the information outputted by S in all directions has the same content, the information being transmitted should all have the same content, e.g., a newspaper article always has the same content, whether the newspapers are being printed and distributed in the north or in the south or abroad. Symmetry of traveled space mainly refers to symmetry of social spaces. After the source S (e.g., an author) or its agent (e.g., a publisher) sends out a piece of information, as long as the medium of each subsequent step is homogeneous in all directions, the range reached by the information should be similar. For example, an author has finished the manuscript of a book, which is published by a publishing house, distributed by a distributor, procured by a library and picked up by a reader. In whichever direction, the information will travel through these broadly the same steps, i.e., roughly the same social distance. Symmetry of information intensity means that the same information volume is transmitted per unit time in each direction, or during each transmission; the quantitative features of information in each direction are the same. When a 300,000-word book is published, distributed and procured by a library, its information volume of 300,000 words will be unchanged. Its word count will not be reduced simply because it was procured by a library in Boston, or read by a student of mathematics.

The condition for multi-directional symmetry is that information must be transmitted in a homogeneous medium. This is similar to the transmission of sound or light, where if the medium is changed, the path and velocity of the transmission, and the content and intensity of the information being transmitted, will all be changed. When the medium is changed, transmissions no longer exhibit multi-directional symmetry. In social information streams, the transmission of any piece of information is generally restricted to a certain group or region. For example, a message written in Chinese only exhibits multi-directional symmetry in a Chinese-speaking region. The transmission of mathematical or chemical knowledge is only symmetric in a group of mathematicians or chemists. Some information is only widespread among college students rather than soldiers, and some only among workers rather than doctors. These phenomena are all caused by the different properties of different media. Obviously, achieving perfect homogeneity is impossible in any social media, therefore the transmissions of social information are never strictly symmetric.

Since multi-directional symmetry requires a homogeneous and uniform external medium, some additional rules of information diffusion can be derived when this condition cannot be met. They are:

1. **Topology principle of information transmission.** When information is transmitted from S to R, a direct transmission from S to R will be the fastest in a homogeneous medium. When the external media are not homogeneous, the S-R stream will undergo a *topological transformation*, i.e., since each change of medium requires a conversion of information, information warehouses will appear to perform the conversions and pass on the information. See Figure 5.1.

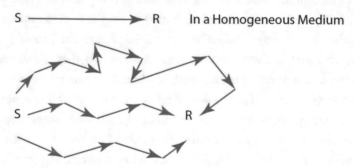

Figure 5.1: Topological diagram of information warehouses.

After a topological transformation, the information stream still has the same S-R structure as in a homogeneous medium, but one or more information warehouses have been inserted into the stream. For example, a middle school class is a sort of homogenous medium where the teacher's lessons can be understood by every student. Suppose an elementary school student shows up a middle school class; he may not be able to directly understand the teacher's lessons (information) without additional explanations (conversions). A new theory by a researcher may be immediately understood by her colleagues, but may require additional explanations to be understood by farmers and workers. A scientific paper can be directly exchanged among peers, but transmitting its information to other social domains, disciplines or regions speaking a different language will require the conversion of information warehouses such as journals, newspapers, publishers and libraries. However, regardless of how the information is converted, the stream always flows from S to R, i.e., the topological transformation of the stream is isomorphic (i.e., of the same structure).

2. **Law of multi-channel transmission.** The laws of multi-directional symmetry and topological transformability indicate that: a. information can be shared; b. information can be transmitted through warehouses. The law of multi-channel transmission, or the multi-channel principle is a combination of the two properties.

Information is both shareable, as its transmission in a homogeneous medium is isotropic (i.e., the same in all directions), and topologically transformable, as its transmissions often exhibit varying structures in various heterogeneous media. Therefore whether the media are homogeneous or heterogeneous, the information should be able to reach the receiver R through an infinite number of channels, and the number of intermediate warehouses can vary from zero to a theoretical infinity. This is the multi-channel principle.

The multi-channel principle is widely seen and utilized in practice. For example, when S has a message to deliver to R, she may talk to R face-to-face, make a phone call, write a letter or write an article that can be viewed through the information system. Many types of information services, including libraries, information centers, publishing houses, news agencies, education systems, patent trading institutions, etc., have ensured the possibility of multi-channel transmission.

5.2.2   LAW OF DIMINISHING DENSITY IN INFORMATION TRANSMISSION

The transmission of information takes place over distances of space and time. Among the laws of S-, R- and T-conservation, T-conservation is an ideal state that is difficult to maintain due to many intervening factors during transmission. The law of diminishing density states that information attenuates in any information stream process. The longer the process is, the more severe the attenuation. Like the transmission process itself, the attenuation has both a temporal and a spatial aspect.

In the spatial domain, we can suppose an information source S, which outputs information as sound at a certain moment. Under ideal conditions, the vibration of the sound is symmetric in all directions, forming a spherical shape. To simplify, we can take the pressure of the sound as a main feature, as the greater the pressure is, the easier it is to receive the information. When the pressure is sufficiently weakened, it will be impossible for the receiver to perceive the information. Suppose the pressure p (which will reduce as r increases) at unit radius $r = 1$ from S to be P_0. The surface area of the unit sphere is $4\pi r^2 = 4\pi$. The total force on the sphere surface is $4\pi P_0$. As the transmission takes place, the sphere surface area will expand along with r, but the total force will be constant at $4\pi P_0$. Thus when the radius is r ($r>1$), the pressure on the sphere surface will be

$$p = \frac{4\pi p_0}{4\pi r^2} = \frac{p_0}{r^2} \ ,$$

where if $r \to \infty$, $p \to 0$. This is why the transmission of both sound and light are limited by distance.

Similarly, we may suppose S as a source that sends out information using a gaseous substance. Again, the higher the gas density is, the easier it is to perceive the information. Suppose the limit of perceivable density is $\rho_{min} = 10^6$ molecules/m^3, and the gas becomes undetectable below this limit. Suppose the gas starts expanding from a sphere with a unit radius $r_0=1(m)$, and a density of $\rho_0 = 10^{18}$ molecules/m^3. Hence the total number of gas molecules in the unit sphere is:

When r_0 changes to r ($r>1$), the gas molecules are still uniformly distributed inside the sphere. Their total number is constant, while their density is reduced:

$$\rho = \frac{\rho_0 V_0}{V} = r^{-3} \cdot 10^{18}$$

When r increases to 100 meters, $\rho = (10^2)^{-3} \cdot 10^{18} = 10^{12}$ molecules/m^3;

When r increases to 100,000 meters, $\rho = (10^5)^{-3} \cdot 10^{18} = 10^3$ molecules/m^3.

The receiver will be unable to receive the information at this distance.

In the temporal domain, as we all know, information attenuation also takes place over time. Books, spoken words, letters, artifacts, etc., will all deteriorate with the passage of time.

The reduction of information density occurs not only in physical spaces, but also in mental spaces. The system of scientific knowledge can be viewed as a knowledge space, where knowledge spreads the most easily within its own discipline, and less so in neighboring disciplines (e.g., management science and economics, biology and chemistry, etc.). A discipline with fewer connections has a longer mental distance from the knowledge source, and thus a lower chance of receiving the transmission.

Along the temporal axis, a process of knowledge accretion is also taking place. As time passes, knowledge that is considered unimportant (data, articles, books, etc.) will become easier to be filtered out, and what remains is the most essential information. In addition, different types of information are filtered out or compressed at different rates to different degrees (see Figure 5.2).

To use some arbitrary numbers, we may say that among all information known today, a third may have been filtered out after 10 years, and a half may have become obsolete after 20 years. These phenomena of "literature aging" and "temporal compression" are also examples of the law of diminishing density.

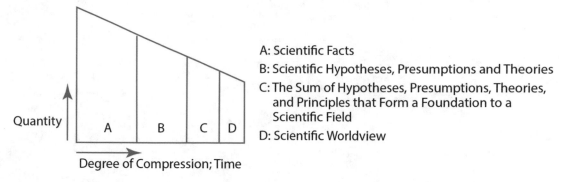

Figure 5.2: Compression of scientific information over time.

CHAPTER 6

The Realization and Impediments of Information Communication

6.1 REALIZATION PROCESS OF INFORMATION COMMUNICATION

The heart of communication is transmission of information, which requires the movement of carriers and symbols. Carriers have two states: **transformation** and **displacement**. Transformation refers to the conversion of information when moving from one carrier to another carrier. Displacement refers to a carrier's movement or extension in space. During a transformation, the symbols are converted from a format in one carrier to a format in another carrier. During a displacement, the symbols are maintained. The actual process of communication in space and time takes the form of four components: carrier transformation, carrier displacement, symbol conversion and symbol maintenance.

Here is an example that shows how communication is realized.

Suppose the salesman S is traveling on business. S reported the current status to the sales manager M, who gave S instructions by telephone call. The communication between S and M is illustrated in Figure 6.1.

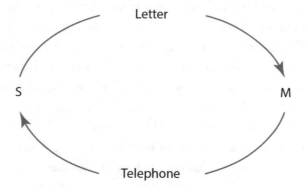

Figure 6.1: How communication is realized.

The S→M transmission can be examined from the perspective of carriers: information in the form of biophysico-chemical patterns in S's brain was transmitted, through carrier transformation and symbol conversion, onto a letter, where it existed with paper as its carrier, and the alphabet as its symbols. Information in the letter form underwent carrier displacement (through the post system) and symbol maintenance. When read by M, it first went through carrier transformation and symbol conversion, where it takes on photons as its carrier, and light waves as its symbols, and then underwent another transformation/conversion into M's brain. We may describe the M→S process similarly. The information from M's brain was transformed and converted into sound waves carried by air. It was then transformed and converted by the telephone into electrical signals, with currents as its carrier. Through carrier displacement (flow of electrical currents and/or transmission of electromagnetic waves) and symbol maintenance (maintenance of electrical signals), the information arrived at S, and became patterns in S's brain.

In the history of human communications, oral speech was one of the earliest forms of communication. It is characterized by fast carrier displacement, which speeds up the communication process, and short symbol maintenance time, which means information can be easily lost. Due to using air as its carrier, oral speech communications are restricted by both spatial and temporal constraints. Breaking through these constraints require other people to serve as intermediaries that connect the stream. In synchronic communications, the spatial distance was often overcome by messengers, or by the source S itself traversing across the distance. In diachronic communications, the impossibility of storing speech means information must be preserved using human brains, and transmitted via speech. In the oral age, diachronic communications over generations were realized through a chain of speech processes over time.

In an oral communication-based society, symbols can only exist outside of human brains for a very brief moment, and for both synchronic and diachronic communications, the storage of information is mainly carried out by human brains. This makes it easier for a few people to monopolize information, creating inequalities in information distribution. Humanity's forgetfulness and inherent capabilities for restructuring information also introduce information distortion into communication. There is also the risk for information to perish along with the individuals who carry them.

In order to ensure information fidelity and realize communications over longer distance and time, many auxiliary tools of communication have been invented. Drums and signal fires are all means to overcome the constraint of space. However, these methods can only transmit a small amount of information, and are still incapable of long-term storage, which prevents them from becoming humanity's primary methods of communication. It was only the invention of writing that brought humanity into a new era. The combination of writing and paper, particularly with the invention of the printing press, greatly accelerated the development of human civilization and spread of social information. Diachronic communications have been made possible by the long-term symbol maintenance afforded by paper, while spatial barriers in synchronic communications have been overcome by carrier displacements over long distances, provided by new means of transportation.

Just as it became possible to deliver information carriers (including S itself) to every corner of the earth, another breakthrough in communication took place in the form of electricity and the microelectronics revolution. Telegram, telephone, faxing, computers, satellites, optical fibers and the Internet solved the problem of speed, caused by the limits in the velocity of carrier displacement, and moreover, solved the problem of spatial barriers in synchronic communications once for all. Modern storage technologies have replaced or complemented paper in the long-term storage of symbols, and both have served humanity's diachronic communications over long periods and synchronic communications over long distances.

This simplified analysis shows that human communications have changed greatly over their evolutionary history. In the oral era, communications were instant and over very short distances. In the writing era, communications were over long periods and long distances. In present day, information technologies have enabled communications unaffected by space and time, which benefits from the advantages of both oral and written communications. It can be said that oral speech created the early human groups, pen and paper created city states and nations and modern information technologies created the global village. The sharing of information resources on a global scale has brought humanity into a huge sphere of information. Wiener considered that information has been the glue that holds human society together.

6.2   IMPEDIMENTS: INFORMATION VARIANCE

During a communication, no matter how refined the tools and channels are, and no matter how much effort both sides have made, true high-fidelity transmission of information from S to R is almost always impossible. Due to the influence and interference from many factors in transmission, the information will inevitably be changed. In information variance, information has often been simultaneously removed and added.

6.2.1   INFORMATION DISTORTIONS

During a communication, the information from S will undergo several transformations before reaching R. These transformations involve: carrier transformations, e.g., the information carrier is changed from air to paper when oral speech is converted into written text; symbol conversions, e.g., translating Chinese into English; and transformation of content, e.g., the transplantation of knowledge between disciplines, and the transformation from primary literature to tertiary literature. The actual content of information will be changed in all transformations.

Information distortion is measured by the similarity between the information received by an information warehouse or R, and the source information outputted by S. The received information will generally resemble the source information, but distortions are also unavoidable. From low level to high level, three types of distortions can take place in as S-R information stream.

1. **Physical distortions.** Physical distortions are loss of fidelity caused by material systems (both carriers and symbols) in transmission. Information transmitted using sound will disappear as the sound becomes increasingly less audible over distance. Books, disks and other media will deteriorate and become moldy, damaging their content. Even one of the media expected to survive for the longest time, the Voyager Golden Records launched into space in 1977, will inevitably break down after billions of years.

2. **Semantic changes.** Semantic changes occur during all information transmissions, including face-to-face conversations. "Due to the uniqueness of each individual's mental space, semantic changes will always take place." In a transmission, the warehouses such as editors, translators, teachers, librarians, information agents, and governmental officials all will perform semantic transformations on the information they receive based on their own mental spaces, which will inevitably cause information loss.

3. **Pragmatic changes.** Pragmatics refer to the value of information to receiver R. From R's perspective, only information it needs is worth transmitting, and even its demanded information is affected by the law of diminishing marginal utility. That is to say, when R's information needs have already been satisfied, the objective value of a new piece of information is still a constant, but its pragmatic value to R has decreased due to other information R has already received. In addition, the value of information is time-sensitive. Scientific theories, technological innovations and economic information are only valuable during a certain period of time, and their value will be immediately lost when the validity period passes. Another issue is that the pragmatic value of the same piece of information will diminish upon repeated transmissions, which happens far more rapidly than oversupplied food or other physical commodities.

Information distortions are common in all social communications. Their main causes include:

1. Technical problems, or other issues in the channels. For example, technical problems such as interruption of signals, noise interference and machine malfunctions are common in radio broadcast and telephone communications.

2. Distortion by too many information warehouses. In a sociological experiment about the accuracy of oral communication, a message was passed one-by-one through a group of volunteers. The message heard by the last volunteer turned out to be entirely different from the message sent out at the start. The published version of an article may suffer from typos, print errors or even tampering by a misguided editor. Ancient manuscripts have generally been copied, translated and retranslated many times,

causing significant distortions. These are all distortions caused by passing through too many information warehouses.

3. Distortion due to social factors. From the very beginning, communications have been a tightly controlled part of human society. Once under control, the reliability of information becomes affected by social factors. In early societies, information on food, enemies and weather had to be controlled to ensure a group's survival. In later times, information from state secrets to an individual's private information has all been subject to control. History is full of examples of ruling classes' attempts to strengthen or restrict communications according to their needs: Hebrew heretics were forced to hide their scrolls in mountain caves; Socrates was poisoned for "corrupting the youths"; China's Qin dynasty was infamous for burning books and burying scholars alive; many Renaissance scholars were forbidden to express their views or expelled from universities; totalitarian governments of the early Enlightenment era often confiscated printing presses.

4. Distortions due to natural factors. Communications are a combination of natural and social processes, and many natural factors can cause distortions, or even interrupt communications, e.g., mold on printed works, deterioration of disks, films and magnetic tapes and even disasters like fire, flood and earthquake.

6.2.2   INFORMATION ADDITIONS

Unlike distortion, information additions during transmission are measured by the information received by R. From R's perspective, a portion of I_S, the information outputted by S, should have been retained when the transmission reaches R. This baseline volume I'_S is lower than I_S due to attenuation. However, the actual volume of information R receives tends to be larger than I'_S. Such additional information is generated by various factors in the communication, such as information warehouses, communication technologies and symbol conversions, and transmitted along with information from S.

Additional information is generated and transmitted in all communications. During a telephone call, the duration of the call, the caller's mood and dialect, etc., are all transmitted to the listener in addition to the semantic information the caller wants to convey. When readers receive a scientific article, they will acquire not only its content, but also additional information including its length, the language it is written in, the name and price of the journal it is published in, the paper it is printed on, etc. After a journalist finishes writing a news script, it will be edited by an editor and narrated by a reporter in a newsroom, adding new information. Some additional information is useful, and some is useless or harmful.

Causes of additional information include:

1. **Natural factors.** Communications rely on both human participation and physical technologies and conditions, and the interactions of physical elements may introduce additional information. Books will retain information about their oxidation in the air and the mold growing on them. Lightning strikes will be recorded in certain tele-comm signals. In an oral conversation, an individual's dialect, fluency, and even attire will be received by the other side as additional information.

2. **Technological factors.** Technological factors are part natural and part social. They may also cause additional information, such as variations in signals caused by voltage changes, or the characteristics of the paper and printer used to print an article.

3. **Social factors.** These are the most complicated and varied influences on communications. Characteristics of information warehouses, such as the guiding philosophy and capabilities of an editor, or criteria for cataloging in a library, will all create additional information. The supporting social structures, such as the government's legislations regarding communication, economic support and structure of the information system, will all be embedded into the communication. A good example is the beacon towers on the Great Wall. At the time of their design and construction, people were only concerned with their pragmatic value, which is to transmit information about warfare on the frontier, and were uninterested in their aesthetic value, or what they say about their society. But from today's perspective, we know little about what had once been communicated by their signal fires, yet we greatly appreciate their additional aesthetic, historical and social information. In this case, the addition of information is caused by changes in society.

We speak of information distortions mainly in regard to the information outputted by S, and information additions in regard of the portion of information from S that should have been received by R. When a typical reader encounters an old book, she will first notice its content, and then on its year of publication, page designs, paper material, printing technologies, state of preservation, etc. That is to say, we tend to receive the additional information gradually.

6.3   IMPEDIMENTS: INFORMATION DISORDER

Because humanity produces and utilizes information for diverse and complex purposes, our communication systems can be said to be a process of entropy increase ever since its creation. This is signified by: the massive, rapidly increasing, and increasingly dispersed state of information; the diversity of media and channels, compared to the high degree of overlap of content; the increase of circulation speed and the decrease of content quality. These features have made controlling communications more difficult than ever. While we have successfully overcome the barriers of space and time through our technologies, we are still far from overcoming the inefficiency caused by information disorder.

6.4   IMPEDIMENTS: INFORMATION FIDELITY AND REDUNDANCY

The purpose of communication is to transmit S's information accurately to R. In order for communication to be effective, countermeasures for information distortions and additions are indispensable. Throughout history, humanity has developed many methods to ensure accurate communication. These methods can be classified into two approaches, increasing information fidelity and increasing information redundancy.

6.4.1   INFORMATION FIDELITY

Fidelity of information, or in other words, the conservation of information, is a basic requirement of communication. A communication can hardly be called as such if the received information has lost all resemblance to the source, and the search for high-fidelity communication technologies has always been a priority of human civilization.

While transmitting all information from S to R with perfect accuracy has never been possible, a baseline of communication fidelity can often be established. The goal of fidelity-increasing methods is to reach or exceed this baseline. They include humanity's many technical and institutional designs that improve the flow of information. Oral speech communications are impermanent and the most susceptible to distortions, which encouraged humanity to invent writing, thus greatly increasing information fidelity. Writing was followed by the printing press, and then by telegram, telephone, photography, satellite communications, television, photocopying and the information superhighway—the Internet. These technologies have all increased information fidelity, and reduced errors caused by information warehouses.

Increasing information fidelity means the prevention of both distortions and additions. The distortion and addition of information are a natural process, while the preservation of fidelity is a result of conscious human effort, and the goal of human communication.

6.4.2   INFORMATION REDUNDANCY

Increasing redundancy is a basic method for decreasing information distortion. By adding redundant information, often utilizing multiple channels of transmission, we can reduce the potential loss of information.

The redundancy principle is widely utilized in human communications. In everyday speech, information is often repeated to avoid potential loss, even if receiving the information once would be sufficient for the receiver.

The following are considered very simple sentences in spoken English:

"He studies very well."

"I am a student."

In the first sentence, "studies" is an inflection of "study." Strictly speaking, the same meaning can be expressed using "He study very well." However, by using the singular third-person form of the verb "study," the information that the subject is in third person has been repeated, making the information easier to understand. The inflection of words is a form of information redundancy.

Similarly, we know the subject in the second sentence is "I" even if we have missed the word, due to redundant information contained in the verb "am." The information will become harder to ascertain if we remove the inflection of the "be" verb from the English language, turning all sentences into something like "I be a student" or "he be a student."

Redundancy is even more commonplace in written language. In the following passage, the information can be understood even without the words in parentheses:

What (is) information? In (a) sense this (is) a question (which) anybody could answer. Information (is) all around (us). Information (is) the staple diet (of) the readers of newspapers (and) the mass audiences (of) the broadcasting media (and) the cinema.

Another form of information redundancy is multi-channel transmission. We may take several different paths to ensure the information can be delivered to the receiver, e.g., by making several telephone calls, or writing several letters. In social communication, media such as television, newspapers, magazines and books can be viewed as the different methods utilized in a multi-channel transmission. For example, important news, policies and legislations will be reported by the media of television, radio, newspapers and magazines. If we only print one copy of each book, or broadcast news exclusively through television, the transmission to a receiver is much more likely to be interrupted since there is only one channel of information. By printing and distributing thousands of copies of a book, or by spreading news via television, newspapers and magazines simultaneously, the chance of reaching any given receiver is greatly increased. In information systems, it is possible to search for information using multiple methods and criteria, which is another case of utilizing information redundancy.

In opposition to the redundancy principle, the principle of anti-redundancy has also been utilized in communications. The purpose of reducing redundancy is to control information whose spread may have detrimental consequences, preventing them from being acquired by outsiders. Examples of the anti-redundancy principle at work include hunting for criminals, important decisions regarding the stock market, single-line connections in espionage, protection of state secrets, etc.

CHAPTER 7

Application: Internet Information Communication

7.1 RISE OF INTERNET INFORMATION COMMUNICATION

Communications are achieved through information carriers. Our history has witnessed a gradual evolution of eight main types of communication carriers: non-carrier (verbal interaction), natural carriers, artificial carriers, paper, film and photography, video and audio, packaged electronic carriers and the Internet. Generally, the evolutionary process conforms to the following rule: expansion of storage capacity; enhancement of information loading method; higher-speed access and transmission; improvement in portability and user friendliness; reduction of cost (Fang, 2002a) . The forms and characteristics of communication activities follow a corresponding path of evolution.

As a new information carrier, the Internet has the following advantages compared to traditional media: (a) Rapid information transfer and updating. The Internet has provided an information transfer method with the highest speed and greatest convenience so far. (b) Vast information and rich content. The Internet contains abundant and diverse information, which is unimaginable for traditional publications. (c) Convenience of search. People are able to easily secure required information via search engines; e-mails and forums and conveniently store them. (d) Combination of hypertexts and multimedia. By incorporating links to other multimedia information into data, the Internet enriches the information content and improves its user friendliness. (e) Strong interaction. This is one of the most unique features of Internet media, which enables users to promptly acquire information, feedbacks and responses from other users through interactions, thus leading to two-way communications.

In the past, the typical pattern of communication was built upon the paper carrier. The Internet has now gradually taken its place as the main carrier of information. In addition to replacing the old carrier forms, the Internet also brings about a more profound influence by changing the way in which people communicate with each other, giving birth to a great number of increasingly popular online communication tools, such as e-mail, digital discussion forums, newsgroups, instant messaging (IM), blogs, wikis and social networks.

According to the *34th Statistical Report on Internet Development in China* (2014) published by CNNIC, the Chinese netizens' utilization behaviors of web applications mainly consist of information acquisition, interaction and communication, and entertainment and commerce (as shown in Table 7.1) . Meanwhile, internet-based communication has become increasingly popular. In addition to traditional web applications like e-mails and forums, people have come to favor a series of newer communication applications represented by blogs and social networks.

Table 7.1: The usage rates of web application for Chinese netizens						
Type	Application	Dec 2013 User Scale (10,000)	July 2014 User Scale (10,000)	Dec 2013 Usage Rate	June 2014 Usage Rate	Increase Rate for the Half-year Period
Interaction and Communication	Instant messaging	53,215	56423	86.2%	89.3%	6.0%
Information acquisition	Search engine	48,966	50749	79.3%	80.3%	3.6%
Information acquisition	Online news	49,132	50316	79.6%	79.6%	2.4%
Entertainment	Online music	45,312	48761	73.4%	77.2%	7.6%
Interaction and Communication	Blog/personal space	43,658	44430	70.7%	70.3%	1.8%
Entertainment	Online video	42,820	43877	69.3%	69.4%	2.5%
Entertainment	Online game	33,803	36811	54.7%	58.2%	8.9%
Commerce	Online shopping	30,189	33151	48.9%	52.5%	9.8%
Commerce	Online payment	26,020	29227	42.1%	46.2%	12.3%
Entertainment	Online literature	27,441	28939	44.4%	45.8%	5.5%
Interaction and Communication	Microblog	28,078	27535	45.5%	43.6%	-1.9%
Commerce	Online bank	25,006	27188	40.5%	43.0%	8.7%
Interaction and Communication	E-mail	25,921	26867	42.0%	42.5%	3.6%
Interaction and Communication	Social network sites	27,769	25722	45.0%	40.7%	-7.4%
Commerce	Traveling and booking	18,077	18960	29.3%	30.0%	4.9%

Commerce	Group purchase	14067	14827	22.8%	23.5%	5.4%
Interaction and Communication	Forum/BBS	12046	12407	19.5%	19.6%	3.0%
Commerce	Online financial management	—	6383	—	10.1%	—

7.2   SCHEMA AND CHARACTERISTICS OF INTERNET INFORMATION COMMUNICATION

7.2.1   SCHEMA OF INTERNET INFORMATION COMMUNICATION

Based on the characteristics of online information environment and the different types of Internet communication applications, the schema for information communication in the Internet environment can be described as in Figure 7.1 (Hao, 2003). The main pathway is denoted by thick arrows, compared with the traditional pathway denoted by thin arrows. The pass-through arrow, which is at the left-most position, represents face-to-face communication without any information agents; the right-most one, which goes to the goal through Other Channels, represents information communication through information agents. The term *Other Channels* represents all channels except for the Internet.

In this schema, information users can be classified into four types.

1. Internet information producer, i.e., producer of original information, usually includes both individuals and groups such as governments or enterprises. With the development and popularity of the Internet, the number of Internet information producers soars accordingly.

2. Internet information distributor, who releases original information online by using information technologies and provides information for users that browse and obtain required information via information executors.

3. Internet information executor, who handles the request sent by an information user in the intermediary process and sends it back to the requester.

4. Internet information user, referring to an individual or group who accepts and uses information, including governments, various enterprises and control sections.

Through the main communication channels denoted by thick arrows, Internet information communication is a process consisting of information creation by producers, information processing by executors and information release by distributors. The Internet involves not only private and public networks, but also other types of networks. Information users can access information through a wide variety of channels. Since it is a two-way process, an information producer can utilize information, while an information distributor can act as an information executor. A user is allowed to play multiple roles in the Internet environment. An information producer can also be an information user at the same time. If one surfs the Internet only for browsing or downloading information, she is merely an information user; however, if she has released information online, she can also be viewed as an information producer (Qu, 2007).

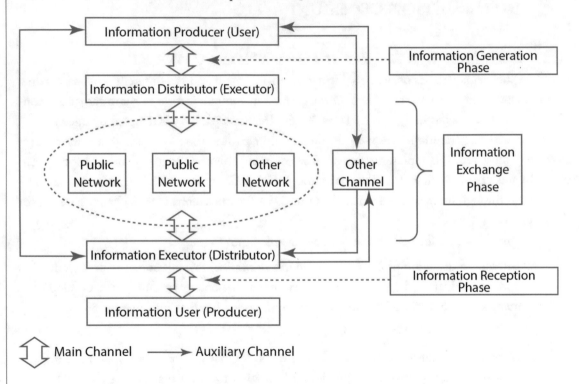

Figure 7.1: Internet information communication pattern.

Based on the pattern above, the whole process of Internet information communication includes three parts: generation, exchange and reception of information.

1. **Information generation phase.** The information is created by an information producer before being distributed on the Internet. There are a wide variety of sources for original information. On the one hand, publishers create, provide various types

of digital journals and offer websites with remote virtual digital collection, together with searching, transmission and long-term storage, forming a widely available digital information resource system. Through the relationship with publishers and libraries, information distributors can access the servers of publishing and library websites, providing users with integrated digital information service. On the other hand, information producers can directly release information through multiple web applications such as news pages, message boards and blogs.

2. **Information exchange phase.** By using computers or client software, information producers and users exchange information via websites. In the Internet environment, all websites can learn from the advantages of others to improve themselves, resulting in promulgation of website features. From the perspective of information stream, the information exchange pattern involves the following basic parts of information stream: (a) Information producer—website—information producer, which represents the information communication and feedback between information producer and website; (b) Information producer—website—information user, which refers to the process where information producer sends information to one or more information users through a website; (c) Information user—website—information user, which represents the information communication and feedbacks between information users and websites; and (d) Information user—website—information producer, which refers to the process in which the information user sends a request to one or more information producers through websites. The four basic processes of information flow can also be recombined into different processes of communication.

3. **Information acquisition process.** Information acquisition process refers to the process in which the information user sends a request to a server either by directly browsing web pages, or via search engines, and obtains the required information through information executors. To an information user, whether an individual, a government or a company, the central issue is whether useful information can be received and selected in a timely manner. Based on their inherent characteristics, the information users' requirements are ever changing rather than constant. Meanwhile, requirements from multiple information users are different, and even the requirements from the same user are not completely concentrated in a specific discipline or field. All those factors have hindered the users' acquisition of the resources they need. Accordingly, the information acquisition behaviors are different due to a variety of factors, which are mainly embodied in acquisitions of information utilization channel, information selection mode and information identity structure.

7.2.2   FORMAL AND INFORMAL COMMUNICATIONS IN THE INTERNET ENVIRONMENT

When discussing models of communication, we have already mentioned that Menzel divided the scientific communications into two types by information carriers: formal and informal communication, thus highlighting the role of science journals in formal communications. Mikhailov also made a statement about scientific communication: the informal science communication generally occurs among researchers and experts. It emphasizes the direct information transfer between the information source and user, including symposium, discussion, report, exhibition, demonstration and visit, which is usually associated with interactions amongst individuals. And formal information communication refers to the process in which an information department indirectly transmits information to users by using literature information systems, with literatures as the medium. It usually involves the collection, categorization, storage, searching, summarization, research, analysis and delivery of literatures by taking the form of formal publications, which can be seen as a social communication activity. The main difference between formal and informal scientific communication lies in whether or not the transmission is based on a literature information system, and literatures are taken as the medium.

In the environment where printed literatures are used as the main communication medium, there is an obvious distinction between formal and informal information communication in terms of medium types. The two communication types have explicit definitions and specialized roles. However, informal communication now faces a relatively tough time in the system of scientific communication. The appearance and development of Internet technologies bring about an opportunity of reviving informal information communication (Fang, 2002b). In the Internet environment, such problems of paper medium as high cost, publication delay, non-real time reports and inconvenient searching are exposed. This is true for traditional face-to-face communication. With the emergence of the Internet, those problems are reduced to a great extent. The efficiencies of both formal and informal communications are improved greatly. Notably, the informal informational communication, which was once marginalized in the traditional scientific communication system, regains its position in a degree.

Other than the traditional pattern, both informal and formal information communication in the Internet environment takes the network carriers as the medium. Information is generated and transmitted based on the network, which makes the boundaries of network carriers vague. Thus, it is necessary to reanalyze the definition and categorization of the two information communication types in the following aspects.

First, there are two main sources of Internet communication information: a. It comes from the traditional formal information communication channels, such as traditional information management organs and information systems. The information, including e-journal, e-book and database, is processed, systemized by specialized information personnel and classified into formal communication information in the Internet environment. b. Internet original information. It is classified into two types: formal and informal. With an apparent individuality and varying in content accuracy and authenticity, formal original information consists of news, information released in the BBS, e-mail and real-time interactive information, which are not categorized and systemized by specialized information personnel.

Setting aside the difference in the technology level, based on whether information is systemized and categorized by specialized personnel, information communication in the Internet environment can be divided into formal and informal communication based on analysis from information sources.

Second, from the perspective of information communication channels, Internet information communication can be achieved through the following approaches:

1. **Web publishing.** Analogous to the paper medium in the traditional information communication pattern, its communication pattern includes two types: formal and informal, each of which can be distinguished from the other based on whether it is managed by specialized information personnel. For example, being categorized and systemized by specialized personnel, Internet original information, which includes traditional web information and that from regular websites as mentioned before, can be classified as formal information. However, bearing the mark of individuality, some personal homepages belong to informal communication.

2. **Internet search engine.** Being categorized and systemized by specialized information personnel, the feedback information given by search engines can be classified as formal communication. However, the information can be formal or informal.

3. **E-mail.** Analogous to written letters in the traditional information communication, it can be classified as informal communication.

4. **BBS.** Comparable to conferences in the traditional informal communication, it can be considered as a type of Internet informal communication.

5. **Real-time interactive communication.** Generally from real-time interactive systems on the Internet, such as IM, Internet telephony, Internet video conference, the information can be classified as informal communication information, without being systemized by specialized personnel.

Through analysis of information communication channels, it can be concluded that Internet information communication cannot be divided as formal and informal communication types due to the scarcity of carriers and transmission channels. However, it can be classified based on whether the information is systemized by specialized personnel.

Overall, the information communication in the Internet environment can be categorized as formal and informal information communication based on whether specialized information personnel engage in the process. The communication in which specialized information personnel participate in the process from information source, to information storage, then to information transfer is formal; on the contrary, spontaneous communication, which occurs among individuals, without being managed by specialized personnel, is informal. But this kind of classification is just based on the process, not the content of information communication. The information that passes on in the informal communication process is not completely informal information, while that in the formal communication process is not completely formal information. But that doesn't necessarily affect the classification based on whether the information is processed and systemized by specialized personnel (Huang and Wang, 2004). The essence of the method is based on whether the information is filtered and controlled. The process in which the information must be subject to strict scrutiny before being transmitted through information systems is a formal communication process, otherwise an informal communication process.

Informal communication has some significant advantages over traditional informal communication in the Internet environment.

Firstly, beyond the limitations of time and space, informal communication on the Internet provided an improved convenience with higher efficiency. Using the Internet, anyone can communicate with others anywhere, anytime, through a series of informal communication methods such as e-mail and BBS. Overcoming the incapability of recording information content, Internet provides the service of archival retrieval.

Secondly, the time intervals are shorter, enabling users to interact and communicate with their peers in real-time with higher speed and improved convenience.

Thirdly, the cost is lower. For example, e-mail provides a rapid, convenient mail delivery method. Other cases include Internet video and Internet conference. To hold various types of conferences on the Internet, users are only required to download relevant video software online, different from the traditional conference that involves many consideration factors such as time of appointment and payment of travel expenses.

Meanwhile, there are a number of problems that need to be solved, including Internet information reliability, network security, popularity of informal communication means, etc. (Jin, 2005).

7.2.3   WAREHOUSES FOR INTERNET INFORMATION COMMUNICATION

Information warehouse refers to the process in which information is transmitted from production to use. It must be a human being or artificial system, offering a capability of accepting, processing and transmitting information. Any information communication activities in the Internet environment, from the simple e-mail, QQ, to the complicated digital library and database, should be conducted through Internet communication platforms and tools. However, the network carrier fits into the category of artificial system undoubtedly. Therefore, it is insufficient to analyze the information warehouse in the Internet environment simply based on the types of carriers between information producers and users. The impact extent of network carrier over information communication should be further studied.

The carriers, tools and platforms, which are required for Internet information communication, are collectively referred to as intermediary of Internet information communication. Based on its various degrees of control over information communication content, it can be divided as pure technology intermediary, selectively content-controllable intermediary and fully content-controllable intermediary (Hu and Wu, 2008). Accordingly, Internet information communication can be classified as the following types: communication without warehouse, communication with expectant warehouse and communication with warehouse, as shown in Figure 7.2.

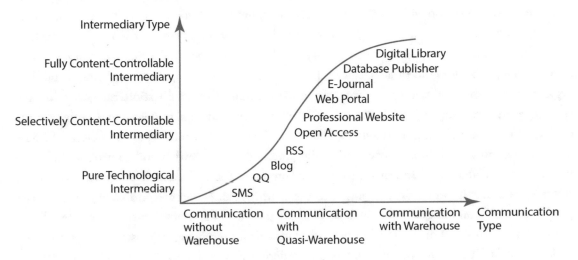

Figure 7.2: Intermediaries and warehouses in Internet information communication.

Pure technology intermediary is a technology support system for Internet information communication, without engaging in control of communication content. It has the following functions: (a) supporting and maintaining technology system of Internet information communication system; (b) controlling the efficiency of Internet information communication (including transmission speed and range); and (c) controlling the security of Internet information communication. Communication without warehouse refers to the information exchange process in which only the pure technology intermediary participates. Providing support at the physical technology level without any intervention and control over communication content, this type of intermediary is generally an imperceptible existence to users, for example, communications through many Web applications such as e-mail, QQ and SMS. Senders transmit information to receivers directly, while using Internet technologies.

Selectively content-controllable intermediary filters and controls the content of communication. However, it merely deletes or screens out information, rather than systemizes and categorizes content. Common examples include BBS, personal websites, blogs and newsgroups. Communication with expectant warehouse refers to the information exchange process where selectively content-controllable intermediary participates in. Without information filtration and operation by the intermediary, the information exchange process equates communication without warehouse to users. For example, researchers publish their dynamic and latest results on personal Web pages or BBS, which is available to other users, or a blogger freely posts an article on his/her blog. In the event of information filtration and operation by the intermediary, the information exchange process equals to communication with warehouse. As for the information processing behaviors of the intermediary, a common example is that a post is deleted by forum moderators of BBS or newsgroups.

Fully content-controllable intermediary involves information collection, control, organization, storage, publishing and management. It offers the following functions: (a) being a collector, organizer, publisher and manager of information, it is responsible for filtration, categorization and storage of information; (b) it reviews, controls Internet information resources and optimizes the quality of Internet information resources; and (c) on the basis of various types and objects of Internet information objects, it adopts corresponding methods for reviewing and controlling information to improve validity of Internet information communication. Communication with warehouse refers to Internet information exchange processes, which fully content-controllable intermediary participates in. Common examples include database providers for various journals, websites, digital libraries, etc. With a whole set of strict practice standards for receiving, processing and transmission of information, it involves quality control and ordering of information (Wang, 2004). With the highest degree of control for information content, it fully functions as the information warehouse in the information communication process.

7.3   INFORMATION COMMUNICATION IN THE WEB 2.0 ENVIRONMENT

7.3.1   DEFINITION AND FEATURES OF WEB 2.0

The idea of "Web 2.0" began with a conference brainstorming session between O'Reilly Media and MediaLive International in March 2004. In Tim O'Reilly's Web 2.0 article published on September 30, 2005, he summarized the concept of Web 2.0 and offered the description framework for Web 2.0. Subsequently, it was recognized as the classic article for Web 2.0, which also makes Tim

O'Reilly the representative figure of Web 2.0. Later, with the rapid development of researches and applications on Web 2.0, the concept and related technologies have been becoming increasingly mature, giving impetus to the revolution of the Internet and a series of innovations of applications.

Represented by Flickr, Craigslist, Linkedin, Tribes, Ryze, Friendster, Del.icio.us and 43Things.com, with such applications as blog (integrating text, voice, image and video into a comprehensive platform and enabling individuals to be the subject of Internet), RSS (really simple syndication), wiki, Tag, SNS (social networking service) and open API (open application interface) as the core, Web 2.0 is the new generation Internet model based on new theories and technologies including Six Degrees, XML and Ajax. All the new Internet applications can be distinguished as Web 2.0 from those associated with Web 1.0 (Internet model before 2013), which is an Internet revolutionary shift from core content to external applications.

As the active initiator and forerunner of the concept of Web 2.0, Tim O'Reilly summarized some key principles for the features of Web 2.0 applications (O'Reilly, 2005).

- The Web as Platform

- Harnessing Collective Intelligence

- Data is the Next Intel Inside

- End of the Software Release Cycle

- Lightweight Programming Models

- Software Above the Level of a Single Device

- Rich User Experiences

Web 2.0 is developed based on Web 1.0, but greatly differing from Web 1.0 in forms and features, as shown in Table 7.2.

Table 7.2: Comparison between Web 2.0 and Web 1.0 (Wang and Song, 2006)		
	Web 1.0	**Web 2.0**
Development time	1993 to 2003	Since 2003
Application foundation	Operating system	Browser or desktop software
Model	It only allows users to read from the Internet and passively receive information	The Read-Write Web, which enables users to actively participate in information on creation
Goal of information dissemination	It meets the commonly shared demands of as many users as possible	It meets the individual demands of as many users as possible
Information interaction mode	Website to user	Mass-scale content interactive communication through P2P mode
Content pattern	Static page	Dynamic publishing and recording
Browsing method	Browser	In combination with browser, RSS reader and many other web-based tools, it is more like an application than a web page.
Architecture	Client/Server	Web service system
Content creator	Web page maker and designer	Anybody
Opinion leader	Technology elite class	Grassroots, a great number of amateurs
Internet value-added base points	Information processing	Deepening services

The transformation from Web 1.0 to Web 2.0 model is a process from pure *reading* to *writing* and *shared creation*, from merely allowing users to passively receive information to letting them actively create Internet information. The goal of information dissemination has changed from meeting the common demands in Web 1.0 era toward the individual demands of Web 2.0. The interaction mode has changed from simple website-to-user to interactive communication such as Peer-to-Peer (P2P) and mass collaboration. The primary unit of content has evolved from static web pages to dynamically published and recorded information. Browsing method shifts from Internet browser to diversified applications including a wide variety of browsers and RSS readers. Architecture changes from Client/Server Architecture to Web Services Architecture. Ordinary users improve their involvement in content creation, replacing web page designers and programmers with the power of discourse moving toward grassroots members from the elite classes. The Internet value addition is gradually transforming from singular information processing in the Web 1.0 era to improved, deepened services in the Web 2.0 era.

The core philosophy of Web 2.0 can be summarized as three values: freedom, openness and sharing. Freedom is the premise of individuality, openness is the basis of self-organization, and sharing is the core of a holographic system. Web 2.0 represents the development trend for future Internet, bringing in a theoretical advancement with unique features of decentralization, openness, sharing, collaborative creation of information, self-organized collaboration and re-mixability.

1. **Decentralization.** Decentralization is the most prominent feature of Web 2.0. With the typical Web 2.0 applications, humans are brought to a new height, each one being treated as an equal subject. They can receive and create information at the same time. The uncertainty of those scattered subjects of communication enables Web 2.0 applications as blogs, SNS and wikis to be decentralized, which also underlies the characteristics of Web 2.0 era: openness and sharing.

2. **Openness and sharing.** Available for all grassroots users, Web 2.0 services encourage users to realize an open discussion and create a culture for information-sharing, continually enriching the utilization experiences of users and resources of websites. For example, users can secure existing video resources on video sharing websites. Meanwhile, they can create and upload video clips to share them with other users.

3. **Collaborative creation of information.** Built on an architecture that allows users to increase their involvement and make their own contribution, Web 2.0 achieves a shift from Read Only to Read-Write. As for involvement of users, on the one hand, it is embodied in encouraging users to participate in network construction and making Website services more appealing; on the other hand, users' involvement is improved through open API. With more active participation and higher contribution of users, a benign ecological network, is formed, which improves the performance and competitiveness of Web 2.0 services.

4. **Self-organized collaboration.** Web 2.0 functions as a self-organized system. Interactive activities between individuals, between information contents generated by individuals, and between groups of individuals lead to emergence of a wide variety of self-organized Internet groups with common features through diverse Tags, RSS feeds. Therefore, Web 2.0 exerts an effect of self-organized collaboration on the Internet. Through the self-organizing pattern, it breathes life into user experience, content and applications.

5. **Re-mixability.** With the improvement in quantity, quality and diversity of information, users expect to obtain new tools to effectively access and manage the complicated information stream. With a number of access approaches and integration modes aiming at multiple data formats and tools, users can seamlessly access all digital content resources, process all types of contents before recombining and reintegrating the content in order to create new services and applications. For example, the Google Maps (GMiF) API, offered by famous photo sharing Website Flickr, is a mash-up of Flickr, Google Maps and Google Earth, which allows users to post a Flickr photo on a Google map, or in the Google Earth address related to that photo.

7.3.2   COMMUNICATION TOOLS AND APPLICATIONS OF WEB 2.0

Web 2.0 represents a new era, a new environment for information communication, with a theme of openness and communication. In the new communication environment, new tools and applications include blogs, podcasting, RSS, wikis, Tag and SNS, etc.

1. **Blog**. Blog is the abbreviation of weblog, which is a kind of personal web page that enables users to post articles in diary form with commentaries. It allows individuals and groups to record and update information in chronological order. A blogger is not only the creator of a blog, but also the administrator of its archive. In the wake of e-mail, BBS and instant messaging, blogging is a new Internet communication tool. Blogs allow users to communicate through trackback and comment, together with hyperlinks, thus achieving an in-depth information exchange and communication. The main functions of a blog include information publishing, research exchange and cooperation in the scientific community and information communication within enterprises (experience sharing of employees, knowledge accumulation). In recent years, blog sales have gradually become an important marketing method, with their unique commercial value.

Inherited from the traditional blog, based on user relationships, the *microblog* is a new blogging platform for sharing, disseminating and procuring information, which enables users to post short messages (usually within 140 characters). It is accessible to anybody or a specific group selected by users. Information can be conveyed in many ways, such as SMS, IM, e-mail, MP3 or web page. Some microblogs offer the capabilities of publishing multimedia information, such as pictures, video clips or publications. The representative website of microblogs in the world is Twitter, which even becomes the generic term for microblogs (Wikipedia, 2014a). In China, the emergence of Sina Weibo and Follow5 further popularizes the microblogging applications. Compared with blogs that emphasize page layout, microblogs features a short and simple content. From this perspective, the technical threshold for users is very low. And requirements for its linguistic composition are not as high as that of a blog. It allows users to express their feelings within some short sentences and update information conveniently, without having to write a long article. Through a wide variety of microblog APIs, users can update their personal information in time through mobile phones and Internet (Baidu Encyclopedia, 2014).

2. **Podcasting.** Podcasting is a portmanteau combining the words "broadcasting" and "iPod." When it first appeared, the podcasting file was received on some software such as iPodder and other portable audio players. Podcasting records web broadcasting radios or other similar Internet audio programs. It allows netizens to download Internet radio programs to their iPod, MP3 players or other portable digital audio players, without having to sit in front of a computer or listen to the real-time radio. Users can really access audio stream anywhere, anytime. More significantly, users can create their own audio programs and upload them on the Internet to share with a vast number of netizens. In this regard, YouTube, China's Tudou and Youku are paragons for it.

3. **RSS.** RSS is the acronym for *rich site summary* or *really simple syndication* and is an XML-based format for syndicating new titles and other web contents. With RSS technology that ensures websites to directly send news to user desktops, users can subscribe to their favorite RSS feeds through RSS readers. When a relevant website updates, users are automatically informed of the newest titles and summaries before reading the whole article. Launched by Netscape in 1999, with the development of XML technology and rapid expansion of bloggers, RSS technology has been gradually approved by users and become the essential new technology in many fields such as news media, e-commerce, and enterprise knowledge management etc.

As an XML-based standard, a widely used protocol for content syndication and delivery on the Internet, RSS collects and organizes the news information in the formats, addresses, times and ways that users desire and directly deliver it to computers of users. The websites with XML or RSS tags are capable of offering this kind of service. The main uses of RSS include: (a) publishing the latest information, such as headlines, dynamic information; (b) website profile. Through RSS feeds, the exposure of websites can be enhanced, along with higher traffic; (c) database query. Other than e-mail that actively disseminates information to users, RSS enables users to search information and subscribe to their favorite RSS feeds at will; (d) dynamic management on website. Web masters can easily manage the information and latest dynamics on the website and promptly respond to problems by taking RSS as the mechanism for single-point response; (e) Update. If there is any modification or addition on the website, users are quickly informed; and (f) commercial value. RSS has also been highly influential over online marketing. For one, eBay links commodity information with RSS, enabling users to obtain the real-time information of their favorite products through RSS readers. Of all RSS capabilities, the most popular one is to categorize the latest headlines or contents of a Website for reference (Shen, 2006).

With the subscription capability, RSS reduces the time for searching desirable information. Consequently, it brings an impact over the information acquisition modes and reading habits on the Internet.

4. **Wiki.** Wiki derives from the Hawaiian word "wee kee wee kee," originally meaning "Hurry Hurry" (quick quick). Wiki is a hypertext system that supports community-oriented collaborative writing and also includes a set of auxiliary tools in support of this writing, which can be browsed, created and changed on the basis of Web Wiki page text. As compared to a HTML page, users can change, release and update a wiki page much more conveniently. Meanwhile, wikis support community-oriented collaborative writing and provide necessary help for writers, which enable wiki writers to be extended into a community using simple communication tools offered by wikis. Compared with other hypertext systems, Wiki is known for its convenience in use and openness. With a wiki system, we can share knowledge in an area within a community (Wu, 2006). For example, the famous Wikipedia (www.wikipedia.org) provides an open, interactive, large-scale wiki platform. Baidu Baike (www.baike.baidu.com) is another knowledge-sharing platform on the basis of the wiki mode.

5. **Tag.** A tag, also known as a label, is a kind of classification system or a keyword attached to an object on the Internet (such as blogs, pictures, songs, or videos). Users can freely choose some words as tags to describe and summarize the object conveniently, without having to follow the existing classification mode. The international websites del.icio.us and Flickr, together with China's Douban (www.douban.com) and Tudou (www.tudou.com), are typical examples for use of tags. Ordinary keyword search only allows users to search a keyword that has been already mentioned in an article. But tags enable a non-existent keyword in an article to be assigned as a label in support of annotation and search. Tags are available for displaying diversified information resources, syndicating, collaboratively filtering and recommending resources. Enriching user experiences, tags are widely used in many areas such as news classification, special subject operation of forums and establishment of tag-based websites (Si, 2009).

Not limited to classification, tags also have a capability of conveying users' opinions, daily experiences and feelings to share with others. Through the same tags, users can search out others' blogs, bookmarks, pictures and files in connection with them. The utilization of tags reshapes the way of organizing and using information. As a new means for users to share resources and communicate with each other, tags draw a great deal of attention.

6. **SNS.** SNS is an abbreviation of *social network service* or *social network software*. As a typical Web 2.0-based application service that helps people to build a social network, the main function of SNS is to provide an Internet social platform that allows people with the same interests to interact and communicate with each other. Encompassing all kinds of social networking-centric services, it became a hot field in the development of the Internet. Many famous social networks have emerged globally, such as Myspace and Facebook in the U.S., Bebo and Xing in Europe, Mixi in Japan and Renren and Kaixin001 in China. In March 2009, Nielsen, an Internet traffic measurement company in the U.S., reported that the membership community with the dual functions of social networking and blogging has occupied two thirds of the total number of Internet users, overtaking e-mail to become the fourth most popular Internet service in the world and growing at a speed that is twice as fast as other four Internet services (search, Web portals, computer software and e-mail). As one of the typical applications of Web 2.0, inheriting its basic ideas—interaction, sharing, and relationship—SNS provides a new approach for information communication and sharing and gradually has become the important platform for information dissemination, giving birth to the concept of *social media*.

SNS is developed based on the theories of Six Degrees of Separation and Rule of 150. The term "Six Degrees of Separation" is coined by the famous social psychologist Stanley Milgram in the U.S. in the 1960s. The theory shows that the social distance between you and anyone is six people, or you can connect anyone through six people at most. It also indicates that a weak link relationship exerts a powerful effect, despite a prevalent phenomenon in society. The theory can be used for analyzing the information dissemination effect arising from weak links.

The term "Rule of 150 "was proposed by Malcom Glawell in his article "The Tipping Point." The theory limits group size to 150 in which you will not feel embarrassed at an unexpected gathering. The Rule of 150 is widely used in reality, as a maximum of 150 numbers can be stored in China Mobile's M-ZONE SIM card, an account of Microsoft MSN can relate with 150 contacts at most. The number 150 is the upper limit that ensures a stable inter-personal relationship can be maintained. No matter which social networks are used for building strong links with people, those strong links still conform to the Rule of 150. It is also consistent with the 80/20 rule, meaning that 80% of social activities may be occupied by 150 strong links (Shi and Yuan, 2009).

7.3.3   IMPACT OF WEB 2.0 OVER INTERNET INFORMATION COMMUNICATION

As a new communication environment, Web 2.0 imposes a significant impact on Internet information communication, which mainly includes the following.

Firstly, the subject of the information stream changes. In the traditional Internet environment, the information stream is mainly based on the websites of traditional media. The subject of the information stream is still exclusive to traditional elites, who seize the power of discourse in such key areas as media, politics and economics, and instill elite consciousness in social value. However, voices of the masses are stifled by the torrent of mainstream social value. The opportunity to create a traditional encyclopedia is only available to a handful qualified people, with a closed elite writing culture as the composition guidance and a super high threshold for most people. In contrast, Wikipedia incorporates an idea of openness into its guidance principle on content editing. With low threshold and broad boundaries of content, Wikipedia allows anybody to engage in writing, with all items being enriched and improved continuously. Every reader acts as both writer and information sharer.

Due to the transition of information subject, the subject behaviors of Internet communication change accordingly, with a decline in reading and an improvement in writing. Internet subject endows the Internet with more capabilities of information output, while still using the Internet as a channel of acquiring information. New information is disseminated online after being identified, understood and filtered, carrying an expression of multiple subject consciousness.

Secondly, multiple information channels and complicated feedback mechanisms arise. The feedback mechanism of traditional information communication works in a tree structure. As the original cause for syndicating information, a root node, including news, book reviews and film reviews, brings about many replies below in a cascade graph with leaf nodes. While in the Web 2.0 environment, except the above mode, the continuous feedback in information construction becomes the new phenomenon. Each piece of information is not merely the brainchild of an intellectual body. In the process, an information source usually switches over to an information sink, with the dual-way information output and improved interaction that blur the border between the two roles. As for interaction mechanism, Web 1.0 focuses on human-computer interaction, with emphasis on the information acquisition behavior of human beings; Web 2.0 era offers a user experience featuring human-human interaction.

Thirdly, an information source in information communication switches from individuals to the masses. As the individual consciousness of netizens grows, a new emotional need for belonging to a networking group emerges, which leads to netizens' dependence on the Internet, i.e., network adhesiveness. Web 2.0-based applications provide practical, true support for that need. Generally, bloggers are desperately in need of joining a blog group. Blogs display not only simple diaries and logs, but also individual thoughts and experiences in chronological order. Through blogging communication, inter-personal relationships and common trust can be built among bloggers. Interactions between individuals gradually develop into a large-scale, massive social network. Thus network effect is constructed and brought into full play, resulting in a snowball effect on relationships among users and finally forming the pattern of social network (Wang and Song, 2006).

7.4   MOBILE INFORMATION COMMUNICATION

Information communication has a close relationship with the development of the Internet and communication technologies. Mobile information communication is an emerging information communication mode, along with the rise and development of the mobile network, which enables users to access wireless' networks by using relevant applications or browsers through such mobile equipment as Smartphones and tablets. Netizens used to access the Internet through fixed network equipment, while the mobile network has become a prevalent tendency presently. In 2008, mobile traffic surpassed the network traffic from desktop computers, marking a milestone event for transformation from fixed network to mobile network. And the emergence and upgrading of such advanced mobile terminals as multi-point touch screen Smartphones and tablets accelerate the development of mobile network (Wikipedia, 2014b).

Main features of mobile network include: (a) Continuous network connectivity. Mobile Internet-capable equipment enables users to access the Internet anywhere, anytime; (b) Location awareness. At present, many Smartphones and tablets are equipped with GPS (Global Positioning System), enabling users to know their geographical positions. Mobile users can search the nearby business information, create location-based information or find and contact friends who are geographically close to them; and (c) Interaction function. A mobile network provides users with an online participation experience featuring reading and writing information. Users can create their own information such as photos and videos, share and grade media resources, publish comments, write blogs, add tags, and build personal relationships on sa ocial network, etc.

With mobile networks, specific information communication applications available for users include: e-mail, SMS, audio communication, downloading or playing music/video online, online game, downloading software, IM, SNS, mobile search (containing multimedia search, local search, shopping search and search for QR codes) and mobile blogs, etc. (Kroski, 2008).

Mobile phones predominate in the mobile terminal market. According to the Ministry of Industry and Information Technology of the Chinese Government, by the end of May 2014, the number of Chinese mobile phone users totaled 1.256 billion (Mobile, 2014). Based on the *2013-*

2014 China Mobile Internet Survey Report released by CNNIC, by the end of June 2014, the number of Chinese mobile Internet users had reached 0.527 billion, accounting for 83.4% of all Internet users. Being nearly saturated, the scale of mobile Internet users grows at a lower rate. However, mobile Internet applications become more enriched, with an enhanced penetration into everyday life, making it an indispensable part to life of ordinary people and an important development mode to all sectors (as shown in Figure 7.3, 7.4 and 7.5) (The Survey Report of China Mobile Internet in 2013-2014, 2014).

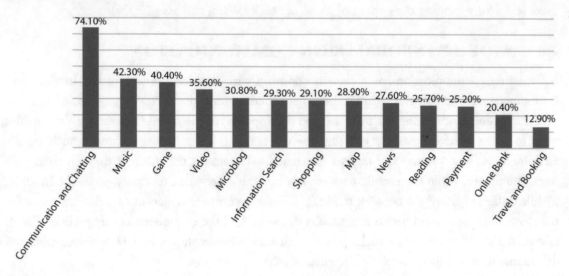

Figure 7.3: Effects of mobile phones reducing computer usage for various applications.

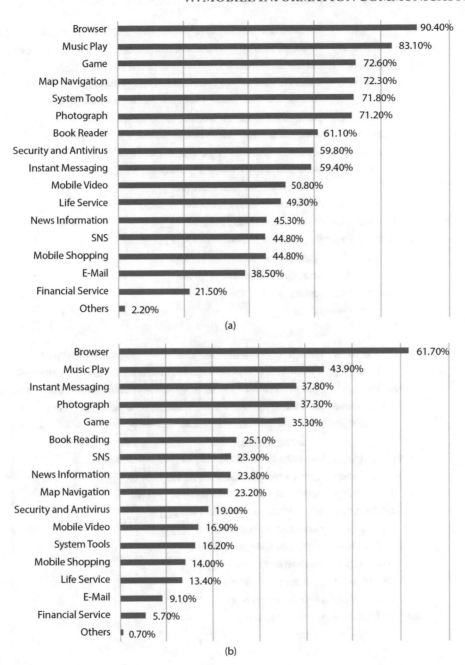

Figure 7.4: Rank of installation ratios and utilization ratios of applications on mobile phone.

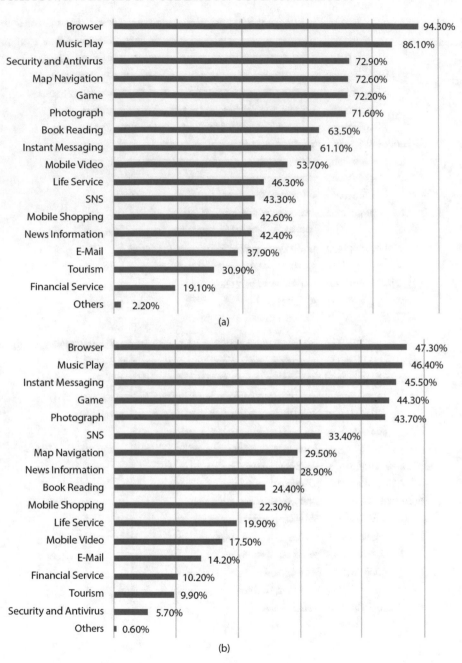

Figure 7.5: Rank of installation ratios for applications on Android phones and iPhones.

From the perspective of sociology, mobile technologies and mobile networks are regarded as not only technologies or network systems, but also a language environment and social model that enables people to communicate with each other. Mobile networks provide an interaction mode in which people interact with each other in a cyber space full of information streams centering on distributed nodes, instead of disappearance of the distance (Castells, et al., 2007). The new types communication modes need further studies and discussions.

CASE   1

"Six Degrees of Separation" and "Small World"

Six Degrees of Separation is the theory that anyone on the planet can be connected to any other person on the planet through a chain of acquaintances that has no more than five intermediaries, which was first proposed in 1929 by the Hungarian writer Frigyes Karinthy in a short story called "Chains." But the theory was formally proposed and developed by American sociologist Stanley Milgram, who conducted a famous test before he finally presented and verified it.

In 1967, Stanley Milgram, who was a professor of psychology at Harvard University, randomly selected 300 people, asking them to send a package to a friend or acquaintance who they thought would bring the package closer to a set final individual, a stockbroker from Boston, since the packages would not be directly sent to the target recipient for sure. Besides, each person who forwarded the package was asked to send back a letter to Milgram. Surprisingly, more than 60 packages were sent to the stockbroker, through a chain involving a median of five intermediaries. In other words, the furthest distance between two strangers is six people.

The experimental results were published in the May 1967 issue of the magazine *Psychology Today*. In the report, he proposed the famous "Six Degrees of Separation" which indicates that if taking into account everyone's interpersonal relationship network, the social distance between people is really short, though the world is large. The theoretical hypothesis is also referred to as "Small World Phenomenon" (as shown in Figure 8.1). In the 30 years, Milgram's theory was never proved through rigorous academic procedures, though it has been verified in practice repeatedly. Many sociologists show a great deal of interest in it, but it is still a hypothesis.

In 2001, Duncan Watts, an associate professor from the Department of Sociology, Columbia University, conducted an online experiment project to prove Six Degrees of Separation. The project team constructed a Website for the experiment (www.smallword.columbia.edu). Each participant registered on the Website and sent its address through e-mail to an acquaintance who would bring the e-mail closer to the target recipients, 18 people scattered in different countries, including a writer in New York, a policeman in Australia, a librarian in Paris. The project began in the autumn of 2001 and lasted for more than one year, with over 60,000 people from 166 countries and regions involved in the study. Finally, a total of 384 e-mails arrived at destinations through a chain of five to seven people. In 2003, he published the experiment results in a paper, "An Experimental Study of Search in Global Social Networks," in t *Science* (Dodds et al., 2003).

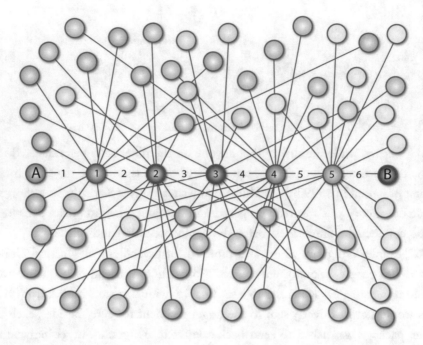

Figure 8.1: Six degrees of separation.

In addition to university studies, researchers from Microsoft also conducted an experiment to verify the feasibility of that theory. Two researchers, Jure Leskovec and Eric Horvitz, selected a random month in 2006 in which all MSN addresses were recorded. Based on 30 billion messages from 0.24 MSN users, they found 78% of all users can be connected to a stranger by sending 6.6 messages, i.e., through a chain of 6.6 people. Later they reported their experiment results in a paper, "Planetary-Scale Views on a Large Instant-Messaging Network" (http://research.micro-soft.com/en-us/um/people/horvitz/leskovec_horvitz_www2008.pdf). In contrast with Milgram's experiment, which merely involved more than 300 people in 1967, the experiment conducted by Microsoft collected more than 30 billion online messages, providing more evidence for verifying the theoretical hypothesis of Six Degrees of Separation.

ISSUES AND CONSIDERATIONS

At present, as SNS becomes increasingly popular, we may consider using the data sample from some SNS Websites such as Instagram and LinkedIn to verify Six Degrees of Separation again. Further analysis and studies are needed for issues arising from the information communication process via SNS.

CASE   2

Appearance and Development of Social Network Site

SNS is an abbreviation of *social network site* (or *social network service*). The earliest SNS is SixDe-grees.com created in 1997. Later, a wide variety of SNSs grew rapidly, while Friendster, MySpace and Bebo websites became the three most popular SNSs from 2002–2004. But it was not until February 2004 when Facebook, a Website hailed for its capabilities of connecting other people and making friends by using real names, was established that SNS really took off. And the complete definition of SNS appeared in 2006. The most frequently cited definition of SNS in academia and business circles was set forth by Boyd and Ellison, who thought of SNS as a type of networking service that allows netizens on a limited system to construct an open or half-open personal space where there is a list of friendly links. And on that system, netizens can view their links and links to associated users (Ellison, 2007). In 2005, a number of Chinese imitators of Facebook such as Xiaonei (later renamed as Renren, www.renren.com) and Kaixing (www.kaixing001.com) appeared, which later were a huge success. Encouraged by the success of Facebook, a great number of SNSs have been created in the world over the past three years.

TYPICAL SOCIAL NETWORKS

1. **Facebook.** Founded by a Harvard drop-out, Mark Zuckerberg, and formally launched on February 4, 2004, Facebook.com characterizes itself as "an online contact list that connects people from the campus social circle. We started a widely-approved Facebook fad. You can find out your alumni, classmates and friends of friends, building your social circle. " Facebook offers a series of features, including Wall (a message board on a user profile page), Poke (a way in which users interact with their friends), Status, Gift, Game, Video and Classified Section (in which users can publish classi-fied advertisements freely), etc.

   In the beginning, registration on Facebook was only available to students of Harvard University. In the next two months, it expanded its reach to other universities in Boston. In the next year, many other universities were invited to join Facebook. Since September 11, 2006, any user could join Facebook with a valid e-mail address. By July 2010, the number of its active users had totaled 0.6 billion (Wikipedia, 2011a).

On May 24, 2007, Facebook launched API through which third-party developers can develop applications compatible with the Facebook platform, indicating the transition of Facebook from an SNS to a social application platform. The rollout of the Facebook platform is not only a technological enhancement, but also a milestone for the Internet to enter a new era of openness. On this, Facebook CEO Mark Zuckerberg said: "We dedicate ourselves to creating an OS which allows everyone to develop compatible apps. Not realized by controlling desktop through managing personal information, the OS is made up of large amounts of information shared by many people and some apps for interpersonal information communication."

In addition, on April 27, 2011, according to media reports, Facebook formally launched the Internet group buying service "Deals" for users in five cities in the U.S. (including San Francisco, Austin, Atlanta, Dallas and San Diego), indicating that Facebook ventured into the fiercely competitive group buying market (Tencent Technology, 2011a). As the world's largest SNS, Facebook has already overtaken Google to become the largest Website in the U.S. in web traffic as early as in March 2010.

2. **Foursquare.** Foursquare is a local search and discovery SNS which provides a mobile app and game. Users can use mobile equipment or send messages to check-in at an actual place. Jointly created by Dennis Crowley and Naveen Selvadurai, Foursquare is a user location-based mobile service website that enables mobile users to share their geographical location information with others. Unlike other SNS, Foursquare mainly aims at mobile users, with its user interface designed for mobile equipment.

Foursquare made its debut in the U.S. in March 2009, when it was only available for iPhone users. Later, it was extended into such mobile platforms as Android, WebOS, Windows Mobile, and BlackBerry. By February 22, 2011, according to a report from TechCrunch, a science blog in the U.S., Foursquare reached seven million user IDs (TechCrunch, 2011). Focusing on a relationship between the human and geographical location, Foursquare encourages more users to join in with an incentive on number of logons. On February 1, 2010, Foursquare reached a cooperation agreement with Bravo TV in which the programs of Bravo TV are combined with the gaming activities of Foursquare to allow audiences to interact with Bravo even after they turn off TVs, computers or stop watching Bravo programs for a long time (Tencent Technology, 2011b).

In addition, Foursquare rolled out a new feature, the Explore tab, that enables users to tell Foursquare what they are searching for and obtain the nearest business information through that app. In essence, it can be seen as Foursquare's recommendation engine. The recommendation information is given based on the check-in locations of users and their friends as well as history data. In addition to the Explore tab, Foursquare also added a new feature by introducing some contexts into users' check-ins in the past: when users review their check-in records, the feature allows them to not only view their own photos, but also those of their friends.

On March 10, 2011, Foursquare upgraded its apps on iPhone and Android platforms. Business users can freely capitalize on these apps after being verified by the new system. They can create a promotion activity on mobile networks and add it to the Foursquare network within a few minutes. Superior to the mode in which business users can only create a promotion campaign each time and new ones cannot be launched unless old ones are removed, the platform allows users to add multiple promotion campaigns each time. In addition to enabling a shop to launch diverse types of promotion campaigns, this upgrade also allows a business user with multiple shops to launch and mange promotion campaign in different shops.

As for the development orientation of Foursquare, Dennis Crowley, founder of Foursquare, expects future check-ins to become more automated and quick, as the service will become more notification-oriented than focused on check-ins. He envisioned a Foursquare that is "listening for what's going on around you … you're walking down the street and normally you eat lunch, but you haven't yet. And Foursquare will tell you that you're close to a sandwich place you read about in the New York Times three weeks ago. And that's what you want to try."

3. **WeChat.** Planned by Shenzhen Tencent Holdings Limited in December 2010, created by a product team of Tencent R&D center in Guangzhou and launched on January 21, 2011, WeChat is a free mobile application aiming at offering IM service for intelligent terminals. With a user number of more than 0.3 billion, WeChat, which is available for a majority of Smartphones, can support a variety of information types such as voice SMS, video, picture and text in multiple modes including group chat, while consuming very little traffic. By November 2013, the number of its registered users reached 0.6 billion, enabling WeChat to become the mobile IM service software with the largest number of users in Asia. As there is a saying on its homepage, "WeChat is a life style," WeChat has been integrated to our daily life and become the indispensable chat tool for ordinary people.

On January 21, 2011, WeChat released its 1.0 beta version aiming at iPhone users. This version supported adding friends by importing the existing contact information on QQ to WeChat. However, the earlier WeChat version only had some simple features such as IM, sharing photos and replacing avatars. On May 10, 2011, WeChat released its 2.0 version, which added a new feature, voice Talkback. The new feature became very popular and attracted a substantial number of people to join in. On October 1, 2011, WeChat upgraded its functionality again with the rollout of the 3.0 version. In addition to the new features of "Shake" and "Drift bottle," WeChat also incorporated the traditional Chinese option to its MUI and became available to mobile users in Hong Kong, Macau, Taiwan, the U.S. and Japan. In March 2012, the number of WeChat users reached 0.1 billion. With the rollout of WeChat 4.0 version on April 19, it added another new feature, the photo album similar to Instagram that enables users to share photos with members of their friend circle who can comment on photos and click the "like" button. On September 17, 2012, Tencent's WeChat team announced that WeChat had a total of 0.2 billion registered users. At midnight, January 15, 2013, the WeChat team announced that WeChat users had exceeded 0.3 billion. By October 24, 2013, Tencent's Wechat users had surpassed 0.6 billion, with a total of 0.1 billion daily active users. By now, WeChat has become the communication software with the largest number of downloads and users, while going beyond main-land China and expanding its influence to Hong Kong, Taiwan, Southeast Asia, res-idential areas of overseas Chinese and a few Westerners. This indicates that WeChat has entered the global stage.

4. **Renren.** Renren.com, formerly known as Xiaonei.com, is a successful Facebook-style social website. As the earliest campus social website in mainland China, it occupies an absolute leading position in Chinese universities. Founded by Wang Xing, Wang Huiwen, Lai Bingqiang and Tangyang from Tsinghua University and Tianjin University in December 2005, with students as its target users, Renren initially was only available to students at Tsinghua University, Peking University and Renmin University of China on a trial basis. Only students with specific university IP addresses or e-mails were allowed to register for accounts with real names. Having monopolized over 80% share of Chinese university students, Xiaonei.com was purchased by China InterActive Corp in October 2006 and merged with 5Q Campus, a subsidiary of China Interactive Corp at the end of 2006.

On November 20, 2007, Xiaonei.com pushed Chinese SNS toward a new area and height by expanding its reach to enterprise offices and senior high schools. After it was renamed Renren.com on August 14, 2009, it made a fundamental shift in strategy from formerly focusing on students to aiming at the broader society beyond campus. As a leading Web 2.0-based website, Xiaonei.com provides powerful, sophisticated Internet functionality and advanced user experience with a wide range of features including log, group, IM, photo album and market to satisfy users' requirements for social interaction, news, entertainment and transaction.

In July 2008, Xiaonei formally launched its strategy for open platform, which allows third-party developers to use Renren.com's APIs to create their own application plug-ins. Meanwhile, an application tag bar was added on its homepage. In a sense, the platform is built by learning from Facebook and replicating some popular plug-ins on Facebook. On December 7, 2009, Renren launched a mobile open platform to meet diverse requirements of mobile users by promoting its mobile terminal. The realization of the idea for an open platform on a wireless network represents a significant breakthrough in the SNS sector, which brings about the common benefits for SNS providers, mobile operators, mobile manufacturers and other third-party partners as well as the industrial revolution in the whole mobile Internet sector.

5. **Kaixin.** As one of China's most famous social networks, founded by Beijing Kaixinren Information Technology Co., Ltd., in March 2008, Kaixin001.com mainly offers a series of services including photo sharing, online chat, music sharing, network storage, blog hosting and interactive games. The founder of Kaixin is Cheng Binghao, a former executive of Sina. Initially, being attracted to its online game such as Friends for Sale and Parking War, a massive number of users invited their friends to join, thus making Kaixin quickly popular. Since its foundation, it has dedicated itself to providing Chinese netizens with a happy, interactive platform. It enables users to keep in closer touch with their friends, classmates, colleagues and family, learn more dynamics in time, share photos, diaries, feelings online and forward posts, conveying pure happiness through a pure interaction.

Component is one of the core applications on Kaixin. At present, Kaixin has already owned a great number of components, while continuing developing new components. Users can freely arrange the display order. In addition to diaries and photos, other components can be added and removed at any time. Unlike the general social networks built on open APIs, Kaixin developed most of those components on their own. And later the third-party components were seen on Kaixin001.com.

On May 21, 2009, He Jie, also known as Angel He, a Chinese mando-pop singer, was invited to become the first singer with a verified account on Kaixin001.com, inaugurating the era for Chinese stars joining social networks. From then on, Kaixin began to invite more celebrities to join in. Lots of large enterprises and organizations also created their official pages on Kaixin. On December 15, 2010, Kaixin launched its self-serve ad platform. With a vast number of real users, Kaixin enables advertisers to publish and manage their ads at their discretion as well as deliver ads to specific user groups based on geographical location, age and identities, etc. With a pay-for-performance incentive, a user is allowed to deliver ads after a minimum of 100 yuan is prepaid.

On April 26, 2001, Kaixin's popular game "Happy City" formally brought out a new feature: Panic Buying. The new feature allows players to obtain real objects through Panic Buying and Lottery using cash in Happy City, which can be seen as an innovative program of Kaixin aiming at deeply combining virtual entertainment with reality.

Social networks, with an emphasis on personal connection, represent the future of the Internet. Consequently, a wide range of social networks came into being. With numerous features, they influenced and even reshaped people's lifestyles by replicating real life on the Internet to satisfy diversified requirements of users. In conclusion, social networks represent the overall development tendency for the Internet in the Web 2.0-based era.

RISE OF VERTICAL NETWORKING SERVICE

VNS is the abbreviation of *vertical networking service*. A website specialized in offering the service above can be referred to as a *vertical social network* site (VSN), which can be defined as a communication platform featuring a theme. By enabling users to communicate with each other centering on stable common topics such as interest, hobby and professional, the platform devotes itself to constructing a more stable relationship than general social network sites.

Despite abundant information resources on a specific topic on the Internet, information is scattered everywhere, which necessitates a great deal of time searching for available information or websites. In order to find out required information among an avalanche of resources quickly, visitors expect to get the "straight path" to improve efficiency. For this reason, some VSNs were born.

The first bunch of personalized VSNs include a number of websites with specialized themes: Birdpost (a communication platform for bird lovers); CauseCast (a philanthropy website); Footnote (Facebook for the deceased); my developerWorks (professional IT communication website created by IBM); Linkedin (a platform for releasing and searching jobs or tasks); and Traveler (a travel website). As compared to the prestigious social websites such as Facebook, Twitter and Kaixin, VSNs are usually specialized in offering services to users in a specific sector who share common interests in a niche area.

In the wake of the websites above, more VSNs were born. Through a study, we classify the existing VSNs into the following types: life, business (or work), travel and shopping. Below, some typical examples are presented for introducing the emerging VSN and its popularity degree.

1. **Life—19lou.** 19lou (http://hangzhou.19lou.com/) is an online communication platform focusing on local daily life (daily necessities, entertainment and healthcare) and affection problems. It now has more than 20 BBS. Among those BBS, real estate, home furnishings, style, marriage, fashion, cuisine, parenthood and travel and entertainment are the greatest attractions on 19lou and also on the similar forum in China.

   Of its 5.5 million registered users, women account for a large percentage at more than 69.8%, 91.4% of which are main urban consumers at the age of 20–35 years. Most of 19lou users are young and fashionable. With 84% of them logging in to it every day, 19lou has become a part of their life. Meanwhile, 90.1% of them have recommended it to their friends, bringing in good publicity and popularity for 19lou through social resonance.

2. **Traveling—Traveler365.com.** Traveler365 has been engaging in constructing a base for travelers. Outdoor sport lovers may find an extensive range of sport items, such as hiking, mountain-climbing, rock-climbing, riding, skiing and swimming available on Traveler, along with professional outdoor equipment recommendations, general knowledge instruction and newest outdoor sports guides. Meanwhile, Traveler365 also allows all travel inns (including family inn, mobile apartment, youth hostel and economy hotel) to release ads freely. Users who are fond of travel and outdoor sports can pleasantly share their feelings about travel with others.

3. **Business—Mydeveloperworks.** Mydeveloperworks (https://www.ibm.com/developerworks) is a social network specialized for employees in IT enterprises and people who are interested in IT technologies, which enables them to find good mentors and beneficial friends. In addition to chat and game, it also offers some features and tools, for example Project Management that helps many people to complete a project. Besides, users can log in to Facebook and Twitter through Mydeveloperworks, as well as recommend some information on Mydeveloperworks to the social website above, thus establishing an interconnection among them.

   According to IBM, Mydeveloperworks has reached 0.325 million active IDs globally within a year, with an increase of over 1,000 people every day. It now has more than 600 bloggers and 900 groups, with nearly 13,000 bookmarks and 400 wiki pages. Every month, more than 0.8 million professionals visit the China version of Mydeveloperworks, where there are abundant technology resources including 14,500 Chinese technical articles, lessons, development techniques, multimedia videos and others (Zhou, 2010).

4. **Shopping—Barcode Hero**. Established in January 2010, Barcode Hero (http://barcodehero.com/) enables users to scan barcodes for commodities through cameral phones, and integrate user resources of Facebook with commodity resources on Google search, thus offering up a unique social e-commerce platform. Users can find the fun in sharing barcode resources and communicating with friends. Additionally, comparing prices and product reputation may lead to a more rational buying behavior. Different empirical values are assigned to users with corresponding titles like King or Queen (Wang, 2010).

At present, the apps of barcode hero are only available to iPhone users. And Android phone users are not capable of using those apps currently. After the recent technical revamp, those apps can be bound to iPod, while they are planning to add other phone types. Though limited to some specific types of mobile phones, there is still an increasing number of barcode hero users.

5. **Others—SubMate.com**. Launched in 2010 in France, SubMate.com (http://www.submate.com) has dedicated itself to offering subway passengers with opportunities to find somebody and something new on their routes. After logging in to SubMate, users can choose their cities (from a limited number of options including London, Paris, New York, Hong Kong and four cities in Spain: Barcelona, Bilbao, Madrid and Valencia), input starting station, destination station, ride time(for example, midnight, morning, noon, afternoon and night), then find their own subway circles. With this feature, SubMate embarked on its SNS journey (NetEase Technology, 2010).

Besides, SubMate can be bound to Twitter and Facebook, offering a great convenience for user login. Though limited to subway passengers, it would have a number of loyal users after gaining popularity, leading to strong network adhesiveness for users.

LONG-TAIL EFFECT OF VSN

The number of VSN users still remains relatively low, as VSNs only emerged not too long ago. However, the total number of users for diversified VSNs can be comparable to the prevailing comprehensive website, which embodies the theory of long tail effect.

The term *long tail* was coined by Chris Anderson in his *Wired* article to describe a specific economic mode such as Amazon.com and Netflix. Its basic principles can be described as follows: as long as there are enough marketing channels, sales of niche products can be comparable to those of mainstream products. In other words, numerous niche markets can be gathered to form a giant market equivalent to the mainstream. Additionally, long tail can be applied to a wide range of areas such as the Internet, entertainment and media, as well as even VSNs, instead of merely economic areas. Being oriented to users sharing common interests, VSNs aim at offering different communication platforms for diversified interests. Though the user value for a single website is not high, VSNs can gain a considerable development momentum by gathering numerous niche groups.

DEVELOPMENT TRENDS OF SOCIAL NETWORKS

Based on the analysis above, by offering a wide range of information and services customary for users, comprehensive social websites will remain attractive. Meanwhile, users can choose what they really want from various VSNs, thus making up a great number of page views for this kind of website. Thus, the long tail effect of social websites becomes increasingly prominent. To meet all depth and breadth requirements of users, the future social websites will become more structured, with focusing on specific themes and involving an extensive range of areas.

As the pace of life becomes increasingly fast, to effectively use any spare moment and break the geographical limitation for accessing networks, users are gradually moving from fixed terminals to mobile devices to continue their social activities. As a main communication tool with a capability of accessing social websites anytime, mobile phones gain an upper hand on convenience compared with PCs. According to the latest data from iResearch, from the first quarter in 2012 to the third quarter in 2014, the market size of the Chinese mobile Internet grew steadily, increasing from 10.2 billion yuan to 51.56 billion yuan (I Research, 2014). With an increasing number of mobile Internet users, a solid foundation was laid for realization of social networks featuring mobile terminals and fragmented information.

ISSUES AND CONSIDERATIONS

With the development of networking technologies and upgrading of communication tools, people's demand for information has grown, resulting in increasingly frequent and diversified communication behaviors. The booming of social websites provides people with a more colored platform for information exchange and interpersonal communication. In addition to user experiences, we can make a further study on functions, features, information communication modes and construction and maintenance of interpersonal relationships by combining the relevant data and behavior logs such as friend status, publishing log and sharing on some social websites (including Renren and Kaixin, etc.) from the perspective of research. And we can also study the privacy issues that these kinds of services bring, and the roles that warehouses and intermediary agents might eventually play in these communication environments.

CASE 3

Wikipedia: Collaborative Communication

Wikipedia is a collaborative, wiki-based, global, multilingual encyclopedia writing project (Wikipedia, 2011b). It is also an Internet encyclopedia website, with a mission of offering a free encyclopedia for all people—a dynamic, editable global knowledge body shown in the language that the user chooses.

Rolled out on January 13, 2001, and formally established on January 15, 2001, Wikipedia is run by the Wikimedia Foundation.

By September 2014, the English version of Wikipedia had more than 4.7 million entries, ranking first on number of entries among all Wikipedia versions in 276 languages that totally contribute to 33.5 million entries. More than 1.91 million people have registered Wikipedia accounts and have edited it for 10 times at least, with Wikipedia reporting approximately 10 million edit counts every month (Wikimedia Statistics, 2002). According to the rank of website traffic from the famous Alexa, Wikipedia is the seventh largest website and the largest ad-free website in the world.

Anybody can read or modify most Wikipedia pages using browsers. And the popularization of Wikipedia gave rise to other projects, for example, Wikinews, Wikibooks, etc.

Wikipedia is also a Wiki-style project. More specifically, it is the first Wiki-based, collaborative encyclopedia writing project. Available to anybody, it is an open encyclopedia enabling third parties to replicate or modify its content, while allowing people from different sectors to search for information and continuously expand their knowledge to enrich themselves. Before 2009, under the terms of GNU Free Documentation License, any or all information had been released on Wikipedia, which defined itself as an encyclopedia encompassing all knowledge areas, instead of a dictionary, an Internet forum or any other commercial website. On May 21, 2009, the Wikimedia Foundation board of trustees decided to replace the former license with Creative Commons Attribution/Share-Alike License (CC-BY-SA). The decision came into effect on June 15, 2009.

At present, all Wikipedia content is collaboratively written by worldwide volunteers, known as Wikipedians. Without any qualification threshold, any Wikipedian can make their contribution as long as they can write out entries and articles for specific knowledge. It means anybody at any age, from any culture and any social background, can write Wikipedia entries. Everybody can freely add information, reference sources or annotations under the editorial policy, standards and principles of Wikipedia. Any substandard or controversial information may be removed. With a vast number of enthusiastic Wikipedians, the website has become the world's largest online encyclopedia.

It is needless for Wikipedians to worry about making errors in adding information, because other editors can correct errors in time. Besides, the Wikipedia software is well designed to enable users to easily correct errors and edit entries. People are welcome to join all Wikipedia projects in the world and edit items collaboratively in order to make contributions in expanding the knowledge base of Wikipedia.

ISSUES AND CONSIDERATIONS

We can log in to Wikipedia (www.wikipedia.org), browse the terms and entries of interest in Chinese and English respectively, and understand the functionality and theory of Wikipedia. By clicking such buttons as "Read," "Edit" and "View history," we can browse relevant information on a Wikipedia page, with some potential problems: how are Wikipedia entries produced? Which operations can users (including viewers and writers) perform? Users can also edit an existing entry or create a new entry. What's more, readers can consider what such sources mean for the roles of experts versus a lot of general-knowledge writers.

CASE   4

A New Network Communication Tool: The Microblog

Microblog is the combination of two terms: *micro* and *blog*. Based on interpersonal relationships of users, it is a platform for sharing, disseminating and acquiring information, which allows users to construct their own communities featuring a 140-character limit and real-time information sharing through Web, WAP-based and other terminals. A microblog differs from a traditional blog in that its content is smaller in the size of the aggregated file (such as text, audio and video) and its speed is higher in information dissemination.

In 2006, Obvious, a company in San Francisco, launched Twitter, a Web 2.0-based, interactive microblog-style platform. Having played an important role in presidential campaigns in 2008, Twitter quickly became popular among a huge number of netizens. According to relevant public data, by February 2014, Twitter had accumulated one billion registered users. According to Global Language Monitor, a language assessment company, Twitter was the hottest English word in 2009. The Twitter fad also reignited Chinese people's enthusiasm for microblogs. In August 2009, China's largest portal website Sina became the first microblog service provider among all portal websites in China by rolling out the beta version of Sina Weibo. From then on, microblogs officially came into focus in China.

THE GREATEST MICROBLOG: TWITTER (Baidu Encyclopedia, 2011b)

Twitter is a variation of instant messaging, which allows users to send their latest thoughts to mobile phones and personalized networking groups, not merely individuals. In 2006, a company founded by the forerunner of blogging technology Evan Williams who had established blogger. com, launched Twitter. Initially, Twitter only allowed users to send textual messages to the mobile phones of their friends. At the end of 2006, Obvious upgraded the functionality of Twitter, enabling users to receive and send messages through IM service and personalized Twitter space without having to input their phone numbers. According to the founders, tweets are short, frequent and fast, coinciding with the design philosophy of the new platform, so Twitter was born.

Twitter is a microblog website in which users can send textual messages within 140 characters. Similar to the status update feature of Facebook, a user can post a reply to the tweet of anybody else and vice visa. However, it is open to everybody. Though most of Twitter user pages seem to be simple textual blogs, it achieves a magical effect by accumulating a lot of pages. In stark contrast with Facebook, Twitter lowered the threshold. Based on the user experience, releasing a message within 140 characters on the Internet is seen to be more convenient. Thus, Twitter brings advancement to information flow, as Evan Williams said: "it is another step to democracy of information. I firmly believe that the future will be better if people can share information more conveniently. "

Twitter is an online service enabling users to send short messages to their friends or followers. Plus, it allows users to follow any Twitter user you want to follow and to read their updated posts on your page. Initially, Twitter aimed at offering services on mobile phones, which is a way of communication as convenient as on computers. Limited to 140 characters, a tweet can be sent as a short message, contributing to part of its attraction. Twitter is a very helpful service to a well-structured group, despite a large number of unorganized users on the platform. If you follow some friends of yours, and they follow other people, then you can quickly communicate with them. Conceptually, it bears an unmistakable resemblance to *DodgeBall*. But Twitter is easier to use. If a user inputs a project on Twitter, it can be set as Private, indicating that his friends cannot view it without his permission, or Public, meaning that anybody knowing his Twitter ID can read or subscribe to his tweets. Notably, Twitter is completely free.

CHINESE MICROBLOGGING PLATFORM

In China, there are more than ten Twitter-style websites, for example, Fanfou (http://fanfou.com/), Sina Weibo (http://weibo.com/), Tencent Weibo (http://t.qq.com/), Sohu Weibo (http://t.sohu.com/), etc.

Sina Weibo is a Twitter-like, microblogging website launched by Sina. It allows users to post messages or upload photos through websites, WAP sites, SMS or MMS. Sina defines its Weibo service as a microblogging platform, or a one-sentence blog, enabling a user to post a sentence or photo via computers or mobile phones to his friends in order to convey the observation, experience and idea. His friends are able to see his updates immediately, share and discuss posts with him at any time. A user can also follow his friends, which enables him to be automatically informed of updates of his friends. On August 14, 2009, Sina Weibo launched its beta version. Later on September 25, 2009, it formally added @ and Private Message features. Besides, it allows users to comment on and repost messages for good communication.

With a promotion strategy similar to Sina Blog, many stars and celebrities are invited to join Sina Weibo and become Weibo users verified by their real identities. A verified Weibo user differs from an ordinary user in that their account name are marked with "V." The measure is also taken to ensure people not to be duped by fake celebrities. But the two types of users have the same functions. At present, Sina Weibo has shifted their interest toward people from media.

A Sina Weibo user can update his Weibo using a variety of means, including websites, WAP sites, SMS&MMS, mobile phone terminals (such as NOKIA S60, iPhone OS, Google Andriod, Windows mobile, etc.), binding SWISEN and MSN. In early 2010, Sina Weibo launched API open platform, enabling users to release information using third-party software or plug-ins. According to the official statistical data from Sina Weibo, in March 2012, Sina owned 0.324 billion users; in March 2013, the number of Sina Weibo users rose to 0.5365 billion, an increase of 65.5% year-over-year. In March 2012, the number of active users of Sina Weibo totaled 30.16 million; in September 2013, it climbed to 60.2 million, nearly twice the figure one and a half years ago. At present, Sina Weibo is the microblogging platform with the largest number of users. Taking pride in attracting numerous celebrities, Sina Weibo has been selected by many of stars from entertainment and sport circles, famous enterprise executives and media workers.

The features of Sina Weibo include the following:

- Post: A user can post messages in a content interface similar to blogs and chat tools.

- Repost: A user can repost his favorite information, along with his commentaries to his own Weibo and by clicking "Repost" (it is based on redesigning the Twitter RT feature, enabling original information to remain unchanged in being disseminated). All his followers (also known as Fans) can see the repost. They can choose to repost again and make their comments. Thus, it leads to endless repetition of the above steps, consequently promoting information dissemination.

- Follow: A user can follow his favorite users to become his fan. By doing so, he will be automatically informed of all their updates in his Weibo feed. A user can follow a maximum of 2,000 people.

- Comment: a user can make comments on any post (it is a special feature based on habits of Chinese users. Later Yahoo Meme and Google Buzz also added the feature).

- Search: a user can insert a topic between two "#," for example, #A specific topic XXX# in a message. The feature allows users to automatically search all relevant posts containing the inserted topic, make further discussion on it and aggregate a specific type of information.

- Private Messaging: a user can send a private message to any users who enable Private Messaging mode. By allowing a user to communicate with a specified person in a private mode, the feature can realize completely private communication (Baidu Encyclopedia, 2011).

FUNCTIONS OF MICROBLOGS (Yu, 2010)

1. **Core functions: Publishing and acquisition of instant information.** For microblogging services, the core functions include: publishing and acquisition of information, which correspond to two roles: information publisher (microblogger) and acquirer. Microblogging is by no means the sole channel for releasing information on the Internet. One can release information on BBS, forums and blogs. But microblogs have a great advantage on good interaction and convenience. Free from restrictions on time, location and writing format, a microblogger can post messages on his home page through terminals to convey his observations, experiences, ideas and feelings for the purpose of recording his daily life and interacting with fans. The freewheeling way seems to be very congenial to busy people in modern cities who are accustomed to using fragmented information to express their feelings.

   The information acquirer who has no intention of releasing many messages can always find the information that they are interested in. In other words, the infinitely abundant information can be aggregated through the flow of information from publishers to acquirers, which ensures users to secure the information that they required. At present, the real-name registration rules of microblogging platforms guarantee the authenticity of information to a degree. If an information acquirer is interested in some microbloggers, he will make a general judgment on the value of the microblogging information after comparing them for a time. Then he will choose to follow or unfollow them. Once a microblogger gains trust, he will become the fixed, free information source offering users a specific type of information. If users can find the right microblogger in a scientific and reasonable way to meet their various requirements, their efficiencies for processing and using information will be greatly enhanced.

   The information system, built upon instant information updates, is more valuable than other information channels in some ways. That is why users are always enthusiastic about microblogs, despite concern over information fragmentation. Compared with the failure of traditional information channels to satisfy users, microblogs can cater specially to the requirements of users. In general, the most important reason for the development of microblogs is to establish an instant communication mode in which one side provides valuable instant information and the other side filters out the information valuable to them.

2. **Derivative function: Construction and maintenance of interpersonal network.** Maintenance of interpersonal relationships may be seen as the core function of SNS,

however, it is just a derivative function for microblogging websites. The interpersonal network can be constructed in two layers: On the one hand, it is an extension of existing interpersonal networks to a microblogging website. The network friends are actually real friends in real life and they just use microblogs as a tool to communicate and interact with each other online. And the microblog features for communicating and sharing information instantly can further meet diverse interaction requirements. On the other hand, it is based on the interactive relationship between followers and one being followed. In other words, a microblogger is loosely connected with his fans through an information sharing process where one side desires to exhibit information and the other side expects to acquire information. Both sides participate in the interaction more or less and feel satisfied in a degree about the interactive mode above. When a microblogger is thought to provide high quality information with a unique style, a loose social network centering on him is likely to be established. Because members of the network have relatively homogenous interests, those fans may interact with each other. Thus, a social circle named after the microblogger was born. However, this type of social circle, which centers on chasing celebrities and stars, only constitutes a minority. For most of them, it is difficult to grow up.

The information, released by microbloggers, is the primary focus of their fans (on the premise that the microgloggers have been already recognized), and is also central to interaction among fans. After interactions between a microblogger and his fans, and those among fans reach a certain level, a close interpersonal network is likely to be created, as long as they have the common interest.

3. **Additional function: Diversified network application.** With the growing popularity of microblogs, there is increasing user adhesiveness. To meet the multi-level requirements of users, more additional functions may be developed in order to continuously improve user experience. For example, with enhancement in product function, a number of features are developed by using various plug-ins:

   ○ Twitter Badges. Users can post feelings on their blogs by using Twitter Badges;

   ○ Twitteroo. This is a desktop software installed in Windows mode, which allows users to post messages on their Twitter pages without having to log into their Twitter accounts;

   ○ TwitterMap. This enables people to search the geographical locations by Twitter Username, displaying users' public messages and relevant geographical locations;

○ TwitterBar. This enables users to add the website address that they are browsing into the Collection of their Twitter accounts. Thus, their friends can view the relevant information on the website; and

○ Twittervision. This is an online application featuring real-time display of Twitter updates on Google Maps.

More importantly, to facilitate users' search for useful information, some search applications are specially developed. A major example is TwitterSearch, which is an official search service launched by Twitter. TwitterSearch enables the latest Tweets to be instantly shown on the website and a user can search information by a keyword which is highlighted in searched results. TwitterSearch is one of the most promising Twitter applications, because it helps Twitter to create higher value by aggregating instant information and effectively activate more information. With TwitterSearch, users can search out information released on Twitter. Besides, the search scope will be extended to links posted on Twitter in the future. Unlike Google, TwitterSearch only indexes pages recommended by users, rather than all pages, making search results more effective and thus creating a unique advantage. Other popular applications based on the third-party APIs include Tweetdeck, Twitterfeed, Wefollow, Twitpic, and Tweetmeme, which greatly extend the functionality of Twitter and enhance the user experience.

COMMUNICATION MECHANISM OF MICROBLOGS (Liu, 2010)

1. **Production: Zero time.** A whole process of information production for traditional media and Web 1.0 involves interviewing, writing, editing and proofreading. Web 2.0 features a communication of user-generated content, which leads to an information production time much shorter than that in traditional patterns. However, the following steps are still essential: editing titles; writing messages; composing type; align paragraph and choosing type for web publishing for the convenience of recommendation. In some cases, users also need to define tags, write a summary before formally publishing information. So there is some (non-zero) time required to produce information.

In contrast, microblogs have some cutting advantages: short content, low writing threshold, convenient, diversified publishing channels and instant update, which leads to the information production in zero time.

- **Short content**. Globally, microblogging platforms allow a user to send a message within 140 English characters. And in China, microblogging platforms enable a user to post a maximum of 140 Chinese characters. Due to the character limitation, usually, a microblogging information publisher directly, immediately conveys his account of the observation experiences, without undergoing complicated information processing in mind.

- **Diversified, convenient and instant publishing channels.** At present, the information publishing mechanism of microblog integrate multiple platforms, enabling users to instantly post short messages through web pages, terminals, mobile phones, mobile networks, IM binding and e-mail plug-ins. Additionally, its synchronicity in update can make a message instantly post on the related microblogging websites. Based on the characteristics of microblog information publishing, microblog is a kind of platform conforming to 4A (anytime, anywhere, anyone and anything), which enables it to be an automatic information publishing device.

2. **Information dissemination mechanism: Zero time.** The zero-time information dissemination on microblogging platform is realized in two ways: firstly, dissemination of information source; secondly, re-dissemination of information.

   - **Zero-time dissemination of information source.** The promotion mechanism for information ensures a user will automatically get informed of aggregated information in his feeds in a chronological order in sync with the updated posts. In addition to multiple information publishing channels, there are also a wide variety of receiving channels such as client software and mobile phones, ensuring users to immediately receive information, reduce dissemination paths and time from information source to users.

   - **Zero-time dissemination of information.** With one-key reposting feature and simple messages, microblogs enable information receivers to synchronize receiving, reading, reposting messages, which leads to zero-time dissemination of information.

3. **Broadcast-style information transfer.** Microblogging communication centers on unidirectional "follow" relationships, instead of two-way, interactive, close interpersonal relationships that are popular on social websites. Based on a kind of social relationship between followers and one being followed, a unique pattern for information sharing and liquidity is established. From the perspective of social networks,

the interpersonal relationship is asymmetric, which gives rise to the broadcast-style information liquidity model for microblogs.

A microblog user can follow anybody at his discretion who does not need to follow back. The asymmetric follow relationship ensures information receivers not to necessarily make responses, maintaining an appropriate distance between information publishers and receivers. The loose interpersonal relationships actually guarantee the efficiency of instant information diffusion. Every microblog user is mapped to a number of followers, ensuring that information is distributed to the segmented groups with each one containing many followers. Therefore, a customized broadcast model in which an information stream flows in broadcast style is built, laying down a huge user base for instant information diffusion.

When the concurrent users (on web pages or mobile networks) based on the broadcast-style information fluidity pattern reach a certain number, it leads to an effect similar to nuclear fission. As a result, an instant information diffusion mode, where a message is sent from an information source, and a massive number of followers repost it, is created.

4. **Social relationship-based information dissemination.** Although microblogging is based on unidirectional follow relationships, it can also create an open social atmosphere where users can also gain more communication opportunities and maintain integral information stream by offering @ (referring to adding "@" in front of a user name as a notification of arrival information) and Repost features.

When an information receiver sees information, he can choose to repost it or not. In this way, ideas, links and other information can be disseminated and tracked down very quickly. A microblog user usually reposts a message, along with his commentary on it, which leads to the information proliferation and a new round of dialogue.

5. **Future prospects of microblogs** (Liu, 2010). The increasing popularity of wireless networks, together with the gradual maturity of 3G technologies, brings microblogs into a favorable position. More instant communication technologies driven by microblogs will usher the Internet into a future featuring instant networks. In contrast with Chinese microblog service providers who are still focusing on accumulating market users, their foreign counterparts are undergoing a paradigm shift in business. Presently, their attentions are concentrated more in the following areas:

   ○ **A full excavation of potentials of information database.** By using the open APIs and an existing development ecological system for applications, Twitter has established an application system to earn and distribute profits. Through cooperation with third-party plug-in providers, Twitter has built a giant ecological system. In conclusion, for microblog service providers, fully excavating the potentials of information databases is a way to increase profitability.

○ **Charging enterprise users.** Incomes from enterprise users constitute an import part of profits of microblog service providers. Twitter began to test its enterprise function and is expected to earn profits. And it plans to provide a new analysis tool for enterprise users, help them to communicate with their clients and build brands by using Twitter. Additionally, Twitter offers enterprise users with the identity verification service.

○ **Online advertisement service based on instant search.** Search behaviors can accurately reflect a user's intention. Since microblog users usually reveal their consumption requirements, preferences, life styles and brand attitudes, advertisers can deliver their information to the target people in the search matching model on the basis of relevant data from microblog websites. Therefore, as soon as Twitter rolled out its search service, it drew a great deal of attention.

○ There is a new developmental upsurge for microblogs with development of 3G. With the increasing growth of Internet bandwidths and explosion of mobile equipment equipped with online browsing functions such as the iPhone, a great number of new network technologies for instant information transmission have emerged. Under the tide, the online real-time user experience is increasingly enriched. All the technological advancements lead to easier and more convenient instant communication, enabling people to interact with their friends anytime.

Through seamlessly combining with mobile phones, microblogs create a revolutionary mode, where users send, receive messages, and interact with their friends through mobile phones, which is of great significance in promoting the future development of microblogs.

ISSUES AND CONSIDERATIONS

As a typical Web 2.0-based application, microblogs have many new characteristics, such as instant transmission of messages and fragmented communication and personal interaction. For microblogs, there are a number of notable issues, for example, studies on new characteristics and patterns of information communication on microblogging platforms, analysis and comparison with other information communication ways such as e-mail and SNS, as well as research on the commercial value of microblogs. Readers can consider how the fragmentation issues are controlled (or not) through links and search add-ons, and how these services fit into the general communication model in Chapter 3.

Bibliography

Arrow, K. J. (1984). *The Economics of Information* (first edition). Oxford: Basil Blackwell Press. 4

Baidu Encyclopedia (2011a, March 20). Sina Microblog. Retrieved from http://baike.baidu.com/view/843376.htm#sub843376. 93

Baidu Encyclopedia (2011b, March 20). Twitter. Retrieved from http://baike.baidu.com/view/843376.htm#sub843376. 91

Baidu Encyclopedia (2014). Microblog. Retrieved from http://baike.baidu.com/view/1567099.htm. 67

Castells, M., Fernández-Ardèvol, M., Qiu, J., and Sey, A. (2007). *Mobile Communication and Society: A Global Perspective*. Cambridge: MIT Press. 75

Chinese mobile phone users approaching 1.3 billion people (2014, June 25). Retrieved from http://mobile.people.com.cn/n/2014/0625/c183175-25195976.html. 71

Dodds, P. S., Muhamad, R., and Watts, D. J. (2003). An Experimental Study of Search in Global Social Networks. *Science*, 301(5634), 827–829. DOI: 10.1126/science.1081058. 77

Ellison, N. B. (2007). Social Network Sites: Definition, History, and Scholarship. *Journal of Computer-Mediated Communication*, 13(1), 210–230. DOI: 10.1111/j.1083-6101.2007.00393.x. 79

Fang, Q. (2002a). On The Basic Laws of Information Media's Development. *Library and Information Service*, 46(1), 17–21, 28. 53

Fang, Q. (2002b). The Revival of Informal Communication under Net-surroundings. *Information Studies: Theory and Application*, 25(4), 258–261. 58

Hao, J. (2003). Information Communication Pattern under Net-surroundings. *Information Science*, 21(1), 57–59. 55

Hartley, R. V. L. (1928). Transmission of Information. *Bell System Technical Journal*, 7(3), 535–563. DOI: 10.1002/j.1538-7305.1928.tb01236.x. 2

Hu, Z. and Wu, Z. (2008). On The Digital Information Communication Mode. *Library and Information Service*, 52(5), 48–50, 148. 61

Huang, S. and Wang, C. (2004). Information Communication in a Networking Environment: It's Concepts, Types and Features. *Library Journal*, 23(6), 8–11. 60

I Research (2014, November 30). I Research network publish the third quarter in 2014 of mobile Internet core data [Research report]. Retrieved from http://www.199it.com/ar-
chives/297989.html. 87

Jin, J. (2005). Study of Theory and Model of Informal Information Communication under the Environment of the Network. (Master's Thesis, Nanjing Agricultural University). 60

Kroski, E. (2008). On the Move with the Mobile Web: Libraries and Mobile Technologies. *Library
Technology Reports*, 44(5), 1–48. 71

Lasswell, H. D. (1948).The Structure and Function of Communication in Society (Master thesis,
New York University). 24

Liang, Z. (2003). A Detailed Discussion of Some Concerning Information Science. *Information
Studies: Theory and Application*, 26(3), 193–198. 11

Liu, X. (2010, January). The Spread Mechanism of Microblog and the Thoughts about its Future
Development. *News and Writing*, (1), 43–46. 98

NetEase Technology Report (2010, June 8). SubMate.com: SNS Based on Subway Passengers [In-
ternet News]. Retrieved from http://tech.163.com/10/0608/00/68K9VF1F000915BF.
html. 86

O'Reilly, T. (2005, September 30). What is Web 2.0. Retrieved from http://www.oreilly.com/
pub/a//web2/archive/what-is-web-20.html. 63

Qu, G. (2007). Study on the Network Communication Barriers and System Optimization Based
on Information Eco_environment (Master thesis, Jilin University). 56

Schramm, W. (1955). How Communication Works (Master thesis, University of Illinois). 24

Shannon, C. E. (1948). A Mathematical Theory of Communication. *Bell System Technical Journal*,
27(3), 379–423. DOI: 10.1002/j.1538-7305.1948.tb01338.x. 2, 23

Shen, J. (2006). RSS: Future of the Integration of Information Dissemination. *Journal of Hebei
University* (Philosophy and Social Science), 5(3), 133–135. 68

Shi, Y. and Yuan, Y. (2009). The Exploration of the Information Dissemination Model Based on
Social Network. *Library Tribune*, 29(6), 220–223. 70

Si, J. (2009). Research on the Development of Tag. *The Library Journal of Shandong*, (1), 66–70. 68

TechCrunch (2011, April 29). The number of the location-based service provider Foursquare
user exceeds 7000000 on February, 2011. Retrieved from http://www.199it.com/ar-
chives/201102257598.html. 80

Tencent Technology (2011a, April 27). Facebook launched the Deals service officially, and get into the group purchase market [Internet News]. Retrieved from http://tech.qq.com/a/20110427/000095.htm. 80

Tencent Technology (2011b, February 1). American social networking site Foursquare and television will explore a new model [Internet News]. Retrieved from http://tech.sina.com.cn/i/2010-02-01/09453822739.shtml. 80

The 34th Statistical Report on Internet Development in China (2014, July 21). Retrieved from http://www.cnnic.cn/hlwfzyj/hlwxzbg/hlwtjbg/201407/t20140721_47437.htm. 53

The Survey Report of China Mobile Internet in 2013-2014 (2014, August 26). Retrieved from http://www.cnnic.cn/hlwfzyj/hlwxzbg/ydhlwbg/201408/t20140826_47880.htm. 72

Wang, J. (2010, October 21). Web comments: Barcode Hero, to do social and business at the same time[Web log]. Retrieved from http://labs.chinamobile.com/mblog/42216_68634. 86

Wang, L. (2004). The Scientific Communication Model under Network Environment from the Perspective on Information Warehouse Theory. *Documentation, Information, and Knowledge*, (1), 19–21. 62

Wang, Z. and Song. Z. (2006). The Characteristics of Web 2.0 and Its Impact on Network Information Communication. *New Century Library*, (3), 10–13. 64, 71

Wiener, N. (1950). *The Human Use of Human Beings: Cybernetics and Society* (first edition). Boston: Da Capo Press. 3

Wikimedia Statistics (October 2002). Retrieved from http://stats.wikimedia.org/ZH/TablesRecentTrends.htm. 89

Wikipedia (2011a, March 26). Facebook. Retrieved from http://zh.wikipedia.org/wiki/Facebook. 79

Wikipedia (2011b, March 29). Wikipedia. Retrieved from https://zh.wikipedia.org/zh-cn/%E7%B-B%B4%E5%9F%BA%E7%99%BE%E7%A7%91. 89

Wikipedia (2014a). Microblog. Retrieved from http://zh.wikipedia.org/zh-cn/%E5%BE%AE%E5%8D%9A. 66

Wikipedia (2014b). Mobile Web. Retrieved from http://en.wikipedia.org/wiki/Mobile_internet#cite_note-0. 71

Wu, L. (2006). Analysis on the Information Communication Mode in Web 2.0 Era. *Journal of Intelligence*, (3), 10–12. 68

Yu, G. (2010, January). The Value of Microblog: The Core Function, the Extending Function and the Additional Function. *News and Writing*, (3), 61–63. 94

Zhang, L. (2002). The Pattern of Information Communication under the Environment of Network. *Research on Library Science*, (1), 7–8, 11. 34

Zhang, Q. (2005). Analysis of Information Chain and the Dimensions of Chinese Intelligence Science in China. *Documentation, Information, and Knowledge*, (4), 23–27. 12

Zhong, Y. (2002). *Principles of Information Science* (third edition). Beijing: Beijing University of Posts and Tele Communications Press. 12

Zhou, Y. (2010, July 5). My developerWorks: Web 2.0 collaborative development of new experience. Retrieved from http://www.cnw.com.cn/software-net-management/htm2010/20100705_200099.shtml. 85

Author Biography

Ma Feicheng is currently a professor at Wuhan University and the Director of the Center for the Studies of Information Resources of Wuhan University (CSIR), a key research institute of humanities and social sciences of the Ministry of Education of China. While acting as a Convener of the Review Group for Library and Information Science and Archival Management of the Academic Degree Committee of the State Council of China, he is also a member of the Social Science Committee of the Ministry of Education of China, the Second Leader of the Review Group of the Library and Information Science and Documentation of the National Social Science Foundation of China and a member of the Review Group of the Management Science Division of the National Natural Science Foundation of China (NSFC). In addition, he is the Vice Director of the Association of Scientific and Technical Information in China and the Vice Chair of the Chinese National Association of Information System, a branch of the Association of Information System (CNAIS).

Ma Feicheng has been doing research work on information science since 1975. He earned his Master's Degree of Information Science in Wuhan University in 1983 and since then has been a faculty member of the School of Information Management of the university. In the years of 1990, 1994 and 2004, respectively, he conducted collaborative research at well-known universities in Germany and the United States. His major research area is Information Resource Management and Planning and Theory and Methodologies of Information Science (including Bibliometrics, Informetrics and Webmetrics). During the past 30 years, he has published more than 10 academic monographs, more than 200 papers, undertaken about 20 research projects at various levels and received over 20 awards.